Tough Times,
Tough People,
and a
Good GOD

Tough Times, Tough People, and a Good GOD

David T. Demola

BRIDGE PUBLISHING
South Plainfield, NJ

Scriptural references are taken from the *King James Version* of the Bible, except where otherwise noted.

Tough Times, Tough People, and a Good God
by David T. Demola

ISBN 0-88270-716-7
Library of Congress Catalog Card Number Pending
Copyright © 1994 by David T. Demola Ministries

Published by:
Bridge Publishing Inc.
2500 Hamilton Blvd.
South Plainfield, NJ 07080

To my wife, Diane,
by whose example I have learned much
of the contents of this book.

Contents

Foreword

Someone said, "It isn't how big the dog is in the fight, it's how big the fight is in the dog." David T. Demola has written something that will put a big fight in you. It is Jesus and His surpassing life and power within.

Here is a book that unleashes an urgent message, is free of nonsense, and is at once tough but full of mercy.

There is a jungle of immature Christians who run to and fro seeking quick fixes, exotic doctrines, anything new to tickle their ears. The problem is that they shipwreck because they have been entertained but not established. This is why this book is so desperately needed. Its message works in the real world.

I love the style! You feel as if you are under the care of a loving coach who makes champions out of mediocre athletes by focusing on what really works and on the rock-solid principles of victory.

This book asks, "How dare we be discouraged when so much has been provided for us in Christ?" The word of God is no suggestion box—it is life! It is chock full of promises that resurrect us!

You will find yourself falling in love with Jesus and the Bible all over again, and the result will be that you will be tougher than the times you live in.

Moreover, this written revelation tells us something that will repeatedly save us in crisis: "God is good! God is not our problem." Armed with this awesome confidence in God's goodness, we can slay every lie, especially the lethal lies of religion. We can move mountains of discouragement. We can ignore the Enemy's threats and focus on our mighty God who loves us. And if we wait just a little longer, His plan for victory will kick in!

I promise you that if you prayerfully apply each chapter of *Tough Times, Tough People, and a Good God*, you will learn never to quit. You will find out how to return fire on the Enemy.

Above all, this book will endow you with a new and living relationship with the Bible and the God of the Bible. You will discover there is far more to you than just the tag "believer." You will see that you have a destiny that transcends talent or opportunity and that you have no time for self pity. You have too many gifts to unwrap and too many victories to win.

You will never regret the day God put this book in your life.

Mario Murillo
San Ramon, CA
1994

1

Confronting Adversity

> If thou faint in the day of adversity, thy strength is small (Prov. 24:10 KJV).

> You are a poor specimen if you can't stand the pressure of adversity (TLB).

Adversities are a real and tough part of life, and we each respond differently to them. Some people fall apart, some people hang tough. How we react to adversity is determined by our background, faith, and other variables. We can't change our background, but we can change our faith and many of the variables. That's our challenge.

GOD'S ANTIDOTE FOR TOUGH TIMES

God has an effective antidote for tough times: tough people. That's what Christ is developing in His body. Tough people who aren't afraid to believe God and confess His Word—the same Word that teaches us what

1

tough times and tough people are. Paul wrote, "Therefore I take pleasure in infirmities, in reproaches, in necessities, in persecutions, in distresses for Christ's sake: for when I am weak, then am I strong" (2 Cor. 12:10).

That's tough! Unfortunately, those things that Paul took pleasure in overcome most of us. By and large, we are weak rather than strong. However, our weakness is opportunity for us to experience God's strength, and it is His strength that will make us tough people who can handle tough times.

Author Robbie Kushner said that when adversities happen, it is wrong to ask "Why?" We should instead ask, "What should I do now?" Let's look at what one person in the Bible did in tough times.

There Was a Widow

In Luke 18:1, it says about Jesus, "And he spake a parable unto them to this end [or purpose] that men ought always to pray, and not to faint." This is the lesson we'll learn in the parable—that we should continue in our prayers until we receive the answer and not weaken and give up. Conversely, Jesus is also telling us that many prayers are not answered because we quit too soon.

Here is His parable:

> There was in a city a judge, which feared not God, neither regarded man: and there was a widow in that city; and she came unto him, saying, Avenge me of mine adversary. And he would not for a while: but afterward he said within himself, Though I fear not God, nor regard man; Yet because this widow

troubleth me, I will avenge her, lest by her continual coming she weary me (Luke 18:2-5).

The Lord didn't tell anything about the woman, only that she did something that made the unjust judge say, "I better do something for her because I'm tired of her continually troubling me." She got action because she was persistent, determined and focused.

Most of us give up too easily when life challenges us, especially in our careers. One reason we do is because we really don't know what we should do in life. We need to seek God and find out what He created us to do. Once God has shown you His will for you, you must follow that course no matter who tries to dissuade you. Pursue against all odds whatever God has placed in your heart.

The widow in the parable obviously came to the judge every day. Look at her situation. She had an adversary and had no income, but she decided, "I'm going to rid myself of my adversary. I can't do it with strength or money, so I'll go to a judge for help." But in the court, she found an unjust judge. Talk about tough times. This woman had to face a man who had no fear of God or regard for man—so you can imagine how much respect he had for the woman.

How do you get a non-caring person to do something for you? You do it by constantly confronting the person: "When are you going to get my adversary off my back? You're the judge. Take care of him for me." Then the next day, you do it again: "Are you going to get him off my back? I deserve justice." She kept going before the judge with her plea, "I want my adversary to leave me alone." To say it today's way, *"she got in his face and stayed there"* until the judge cried, "I'VE HAD ENOUGH!"

Luke continues, "And the Lord said, Hear what the unjust judge saith" (Luke 18:6). In effect, the judge said, "That woman is nothing but trouble. I'm tired of her." To wear out a hard man like that, the woman had to be persistent and relentless. She didn't care what the judge said or did. She wasn't moved by what she heard about his being unjust and not caring about God or man. Instead of a negative confession, she acted on what she believed. If we *don't* act on we believe, it's because we don't believe with our heart what we say with our mouth. We have all experienced an unbelieving heart and a confessing mouth.

Then the Lord said, "And shall not God avenge his own elect, which cry day and night unto him, though he bear long with them?" (Luke 18:7). To teach us how to approach God, Jesus compares Him to the unjust judge, and tells us that even as the judge helped the woman, so God will "avenge his own elect" (Luke 18:7). Regardless of what society or others think of us, as the elect of God we don't go to our heavenly Father as beggars, outcasts, or strangers. We go to Him as His elect and say, "Father, I am your son [I am your daughter]. Here is my problem and I know You will help me."

The Lord's parable doesn't mean we need to cry to God all day and night. Rather, it means we should keep our petition before God, and keep on reminding Him, "God, it's me. I'm your child. I asked you yesterday, now I'm thanking you for it." When we pray and ask, we then receive by faith. But the manifestation may not come for awhile. It's then we face the peril of impatience. The waiting is the toughest part of all. Too often when we need something, we give God two minutes of our time in prayer, and then give Him two minutes to answer—if He hasn't by then, we start bad-mouthing Him: "I don't know why God doesn't answer my prayer."

Have you ever filed an application for a job, and a week or two went by without your hearing anything, so you prayed and fasted, bound and loosed, called somebody's prayer ministry, and did everything you knew to do—and still heard nothing? At that point, you may be tempted to say, "It must not be God's will." Sometimes that's true, but if it wasn't God's will and you were walking with God, you should have known that right away.

When you walk with God, you know His will. How is this possible? It's a part of your relationship with Him. How do you know your wife or husband loves you? The knowledge comes through caring communication, intimacy, loving and being with your spouse.

When two people love each other, an intimate communication develops. This form of communication involves all verbal, silent, private, and public aspects of a relationship. This is the kind of relationship you must develop with God—a relationship in which you can open your heart to Him and cry, "Oh, God; Oh, God, I need you." This relationship is built on heart-felt prayer: "Father, I'm worshiping you. I want to know you. I want to know you behind closed doors!" To know God "behind closed doors" means to know Him in an intimate, deeply personal way. God wants us to know Him that way (Matt. 6:5-6).

Jesus told the parable about the widow to teach us

5

that we should always pray and not weaken. He said, "And shall not God avenge his own elect, which cry day and night unto him, though he bear long with them" (Luke 18:7). So don't be impatient.

I've been believing God for years for some things that haven't manifested yet. But several months ago, the Lord spoke to me and said, "It's time to get excited now because the more time that passes, the closer you are to the manifestation of the answer to your prayer." That was an encouraging word from God that I needed, because I'd been thinking, "Oh, it has been so long." Now I know that each passing moment brings me nearer to the goal. The closer you get to God's time to manifest His answer, the more excited you get.

GOD'S TIMING IS PERFECT

Jesus said about God, "I tell you that he will avenge them speedily" (Luke 18:8). I don't know at what speed God travels, but it's always the right speed—and He always gets there at the right time.

There are things I've requested from God that if I had received them instantly, I would have misused them. Sometimes you hear people say, "Bless God, I got my answer right away!"—and two months later, they had nothing. Many times, instant prayer answers cause Christians to remain weak. Learning how to sustain in faith is what we need to make us strong.

YOU MUST HAVE FAITH

Jesus continued, "Nevertheless when the Son of man cometh, shall he find faith on the earth?" (Luke 18:8).

6

The key to the parable about the widow is expressed in this verse. Jesus is telling us that the people who get through are those who know how to walk by faith—not by feelings and not by sight. It's faith that counts.

Will the Son of man find faith on the earth? Note that the Lord doesn't ask if He will find love. Love doesn't get prayers answered or overcome our problems. Faith does! Love is an important part of the gospel, but it's not the essential part of effectual prayer that faith is. True, we must have a heart attitude of love toward God and others —but it is our faith that moves the hand of God.

The key that solved the widow's problems was her aggressive faith. She was a tough woman in tough times. And that's what we must be to get *our* problems solved—tough faith-Christians in tough times.

HUMILITY BEFORE THE LORD

In Luke 18: 9-14 this is written:

> And he spake this parable unto certain which trusted in themselves that they were righteous, and despised others: Two men went up into the temple to pray; the one a Pharisee, and the other a publican. The Pharisee stood and prayed thus with himself, God, I thank thee, that I am not as other men are, extortioners, unjust, adulterers, or even as this publican. I fast twice in the week, I give tithes of all that I possess. And the publican, standing afar off, would not lift up so much as his eyes unto heaven, but smote his breast, saying, God, be merciful to me a sinner. I tell you, this man went down to his house justified rather than the other:

> for every one that exalteth himself shall be abased; and
> he that humbleth himself shall be exalted.

In this parable, Jesus teaches the need of being humble. Humility brings balance to our faith. Christians who know that their faith is from God and His Word balance their strength with a humble spirit, and it is these Christians who reach God and get results. You can have all the faith you need, but if your attitude is wrong, you will be like the Pharisee. He fasted and tithed, but his arrogance stood between him and God.

Some who tithe are not blessed financially because they have a haughty attitude. The Pharisee prayed, saying, "Lord, I do this; Lord, I do that," and then, "I thank you I'm not like him." He was off base. God never hears such prayers (1 John 5:14-15).

SOWING TO THE SPIRIT

The Apostle Paul wrote,

> Be not deceived; God is not mocked: for what-
> soever a man soweth, that shall he also reap. For he
> that soweth to his flesh shall of the flesh reap
> corruption; but he that soweth to the Spirit shall of the
> Spirit reap life everlasting" (Gal. 6:7-8).

How do you sow to the Spirit? By obeying God. It's like walking in the Spirit, which is simply walking in the Word of God—because the Word and the Spirit always agree (1 John 5:8).

Paul also wrote, "And let us not be weary in well doing . . ." (Gal. 6:9). Some might say, "I've been tithing.

8

I've been giving. I've been doing this and that, but nothing is happening." We've all been at such a point in our lives, but we need to hang on as Paul instructed. Otherwise, we might give up just before the answer is due to arrive. Paul assures us that we are going to get an answer to our needs because we have been sowing to the Spirit and not the flesh. He says, ". . . for in due season we shall reap, if we faint not" (Gal. 6:9). Due season has to do with the reaping coming in God's time.

Your flesh may tell you that you are not getting anything and nothing is happening. And the devil is always around to lie to you. However, if you're walking in the Spirit and not fulfilling the lusts of your flesh, then you're sowing to the Spirit. That's a spiritual sowing which will bring a great crop.

As we all know, even when we do exactly what God requires, we may sometimes still get weary. That comes from not seeing things happen. When you start seeing results, you get motivated to keep on keeping on. When you *aren't* seeing results, however, you have to walk by faith. That's when we're tempted to grow weary. We must stay on guard so we don't get tired in our walk of faith.

Faith pursues the goal. To get a quick answer from God, walk right and live right. Also remember, faith comes by hearing, and hearing by the Word of God (Rom. 10:17). Notice that the Scripture doesn't say that faith comes by hearing a thrilling testimony or by any other means. It doesn't come through emotional intensity, fantasy or laying on of hands. Faith comes by hearing, and hearing by the Word of God.

LET GOD'S STRENGTH TAKE OVER

A typical response in tough times is, "Oh, I'm very discouraged." Get undiscouraged! "I never get any breaks." Make your breaks! You say, "That doesn't work in this world." You have a God bigger than this world. Work in your own strength and you won't get anywhere. Let God's strength take over and you'll win (2 Cor. 12:9). The widow in Luke 18 didn't stand around complaining and asking why—she stepped out in faith and action and won.

Martin Luther King said, "I have a dream." He ran with his dream, embraced it and brought it into reality. There were many setbacks along the way, but Dr. King persevered in faith and his dream is increasingly becoming a reality and has changed the course of human events.

What kind of dream do you have? If you don't have one, get on your knees with your Bible in front of you and pray until you do. If your dream has become dim, do something about it. Step out in the direction of your dream's fulfillment. Most dreams never get anywhere because folks are lazy. We need to embrace the dream God gives us, keep our eyes on its fulfillment, and invest our lives in it .

GOD KNOWS WHERE YOU LIVE

God knows where you live, where you work, where you worship, what size shoe you wear, and how many hairs you've got (Luke 12:7). God has known you from before the foundation of the earth (Eph. 1:4). In Jeremiah

10

1:5, He said, "Before I formed thee in the belly I knew thee . . . ." Because God truly knows who we are and what we need, we can depend on His Word and prayer to bring results even in tough times. But we need to learn how God works.

Look at the last part of Jesus' statement: ". . . though he bear long with them?" (Luke 18:7). Someone might protest, "But I thought God responds immediately to the prayer of faith." It is true that Jesus said, "What things soever ye desire, when ye pray, believe that ye receive them, and ye shall have them" (Mark 11:24). When you pray for something and believe that you receive it, God starts working immediately in the spiritual realm, and will bring forth the answer to your prayer at exactly the right time. His perfect way and His perfect timing are worth any wait.

Sometimes, however, God delays His answer to prayer. This is the part we don't like. In many Christian circles, people believe they will have instant results every time they pray. This has turned off many people because they became discouraged when they didn't see an instant answer to their prayer.

WALKING BY FAITH

Someone might say, "Not trusting in immediate manifestation of what you're believing for is walking by sight, not by faith." My response to that is, "No, that's walking by reality." If the creditors come to my house to take it from me, and I need $10,000 to stop them from doing so, I can't tell them, "By faith I'll have it. It'll manifest itself. Don't worry about it. Just don't take my house. It will be here soon." They're going to laugh and tell me to get out of my house.

Many folks have believed wrongly about faith. Normally, faith is not something I use when a crisis comes; It's something I use so I will be prepared *before* the crisis comes. That way, I'll always have enough of whatever I need.

Also, we need to understand that many times we lose things because we don't prepare for possible eventualities. We need to learn some practical things. Some of us are living a $1,000-a-week life-style on a $500-a-week salary. Someone might say, "Well, that's living by faith, isn't it?" No, that's living by foolishness! The Bible says, "For which of you, intending to build a tower, sitteth not down first, and counteth the cost, whether he have sufficient to finish it?" (Luke 14:28).

Sometimes the manifestation of an answered prayer is delayed, but that doesn't mean that we're supposed to cry constantly, "O God, please help me. O God, I do need your help. Please help me! GOD, NOW!" That's not the style of praying we are to have. Rather, it means that someone who petitions God should say, "Father, I've prayed, I've believed, and I've confessed your Word. Now, in the name of Jesus, I remind you of your Word and thank you that what I prayed and believed for, I'm going to receive." This is faith in prayer. It appropriates God's promises. It brings results. We pray; we believe; we confess the Word; we stand in faith.

THE WORD WILL NOT FAIL YOU

Everything else in life will fail you, but God's Word will never fail you. However, that doesn't mean you'll have instant things every time you want them. But remember, the Scriptures teach us that when there's a delay in God's answer, it doesn't mean He said, "No." When I pray in faith, God immediately starts working for me in the spiritual realm where nobody can see or understand what is going on. "For it is God which worketh in you both to will and to do of his good pleasure" (Phil. 2:13).

Even when I can't see, feel, or understand, God is at work. My Lord assured me that God is not an unjust judge, that God is the God of the elect. Therefore, I am persuaded that what God promised, He will perform (Rom. 4:21)—He will not alter the Word that has gone forth out of His mouth (Ps. 89:34), and His Word will never return unto Him void (Isa. 55:11). What God says He will do; He will do (Num. 23:19).

When I learned about the importance of faith in 1979, I was at the lowest point of my life. I needed help from God. Then I heard, "The Word will take you out." That was a *rhema* word for me, and I embraced it. I am now a different person. My faith in God's Word has grown. I can't deny what God revealed to me The Son of man will look for FAITH when He returns. So I must continually work on my faith-walk.

God loves me and wants me to experience the victory and success of faith. "Faith is the substance of things hoped for, the evidence of things not seen" (Heb. 11:1). I have faith to believe that when I have prayed, believed, confessed, and do not yet see the answer, God is working. When I don't have faith, I get weary. When I have faith, I don't get weary. *Faith keeps me strong and keeps me going!*

GOD GIVES POWER TO THE FAINT

Isaiah wrote, "He giveth power to the faint; and to them that have no might he increaseth strength" (Isa. 40:29). God doesn't let you stay in a faint. He said, "I am going to give you power and get you started all over again. I am going to strengthen you so that you can get back on target and stop giving up and letting go of what you know is your covenant promise. I am going to get you out of that place of weakness, make you strong, and stand you on your feet. When tough times come, put your foot down, and say, "I'm not bending. I'm not bowing. I'm not giving in. I'm going on for God's inner strength!" *God always wants to increase our strength.*

There are times when things will be so tough that "Even the youths shall faint and be weary, and the young men shall utterly fall" (Isa. 40:30). "Youth" symbolizes strength and vitality. If the youths shall faint, what shall those of us do who no longer have that strength and vitality? But don't worry, God has the solution: ". . . they that wait upon the Lord shall renew their strength . . ." (Isa. 40:31). The word renew means "exchange." When you wait upon the Lord, you exchange your weak human strength for God's divine strength.

Those who wait upon the Lord shall exchange their strength for His, and look at the results: ". . . they shall mount up with wings as eagles; they shall run, and not be weary; and they shall walk, and not faint" (Isa. 40:31). God never intended you to be weak and faint. He designed you to be strong and tough. He designed you to look at difficulties and say, "With God's strength, I can overcome them."

Here is Almighty God's promise: "Wait on me, I will

exchange your strength for mine." He is telling you that you can't take on life and its problems and stresses on your own. You can't make it on your own—you don't have the power to do so. God said, "I will give you strength. You will run and not be weary. You will walk and not faint."

We are at the point in our Christianity where we must decide not to be weak and faint. We must wait on the Lord. We must be aggressive enough to let our faith be known and not be afraid or ashamed. God is going to answer the prayers of His elect and avenge them speedily. He is going to come at the right time. He is not going to abandon us. We are going to rise up and do what He said. We are going to overcome.

Pray In the Spirit

Recently, I spent a whole day talking to the Lord. At one point, a thought popped into my head: "You need to worry about this. You need to worry about THIS. THIS needs to be worried about RIGHT NOW!" I continued praying and asked, "Lord, what am I going to do about this?" Immediately, the Lord told me in my spirit that He was teaching me a valuable lesson. He said that He wanted me to do what He told me to do and showed me how to deal with my worry: "When you are thinking about those things that seem troublesome in the natural, pray in the Spirit."

I thought about His simple solution. When you pray in the Spirit, your mind is unfruitful. So praying in the Spirit will overshadow your thinking process, and prevent any negative thoughts from affecting you. There have been times since then when I've been praying in tongues and thinking, "I'm just not going to make it this time. What about this bill and that other bill?" But the Bible says that when I pray in the Spirit, my mind is unfruitful. So, my mind could be thinking a hundred negative things, but when I'm praying in the Spirit, my spirit man is making more headway than my thinking ever could.

The next time you have trouble praying, try it.

The Lord's solution for me will work for you.

2

Resist the Devil

The wicked flee when no man pursueth: but the righteous are bold as a lion (Prov. 28:1).

In tough times, we can flee or stand strong and bold in righteousness. A lion symbolizes strength and boldness. We need to be bold in our prayers, yet patient while we await God's answers.

God's Word says that patience (longsuffering) is a fruit of the Spirit (Gal. 5:22). This kind of patience is only developed through tribulation (Rom. 5:3). But don't make the mistake that some have and pray for tribulation so you can develop patience. Just keep breathing and living, and you'll have all the tribulation you can handle.

The Scriptures tell us that God never faints or gets weary like we do, and gives strength to His people (Isa. 40:28-31). God doesn't want you and me to faint. When the devil attacks, be bold as a lion, trust God to do what He promised, and be patient until His answer is manifested.

RESIST THE DEVIL

There are more people in the world today than ever before—so there is more sin. Today, Satan is busier than ever with all these people, doing all the rotten things he's always done. He's still a liar, still a thief, still a murderer.

Too many Christians entertain the devil instead of resisting him. This provides them with an excuse for their behavior. We've been blaming the devil for most of our problems for such a long time, he's almost an old friend. But the Bible says: "Submit yourselves therefore to God. Resist the devil, and he will flee from you" (James 4:7).

Unfortunately, he doesn't keep fleeing—he keeps attacking us to see if we've let our guard down. Luke 4:13 says, "And when the devil had ended all the temptation, he departed from him *for a season* (italics mine)." He left Jesus for a season, but came back time and again. And he does the same with us.

But, remember, the only way the devil can oppress you is when he finds something in you that belongs to him (John 14:30). That happens when you're not fully surrendered to Christ, and there is sin in your life. Fill yourself up with God, and that won't leave any room for the devil.

Many Christians are devil-conscious. You hear them say, "The devil this . . . and the devil that." To them every problem they've got is a demon. In most cases, their problem isn't a demon; it's their brain.

Now there are plenty of active demons, and they possess many people, but if you're saved and filled with the Holy Ghost, there's no demon in you. The only way a demon can affect you is through your thoughts. Your unrenewed mind is an open doorway for Satan's lies. Only the truth of God's Word can defend your mind from them. "Resist the devil and he will flee from you." But first be fully submitted to God.

JESUS AND TOUGH TIMES

We don't have the power to defeat Satan, but we have a "Name" we can call on that is above every name. When we use the name of Jesus, Satan has to flee from us. He doesn't flee because you pray nine hours and fast. He flees when you say, "Satan, I come against you in the name of Jesus." Satan obeys on the basis of your faith-use of the name of Jesus, not on the basis of your personal will power, your church or your denomination. He obeys because he must.

In Hebrews 2:6-8, this is written:

> But one in a certain place testified, saying, What is man, that thou art mindful of him? or the son of man, that thou visitest him? thou madest him a little lower than the angels; thou crownedst him with glory and honour [that was the anointing], and didst set him over the works of thy hands: Thou hast put all things in subjection under his feet. For in that he put all in subjection under him, he left nothing that is not put under him. But now we see not yet all things put under him.

This passage is about God placing Adam and Eve in the Garden and giving them authority and power over all the works of His hands. There was glory and honor in those first two people. God put Adam in the Garden of Eden to make him guardian over creation (Gen. 1:26-28). He virtually said to Adam, "Take dominion; have authority; subdue, conquer, guard, defend." He gave them glory and honor, but did not put everything under their feet. This sovereign power was given to Jesus, the second Adam: "And Jesus came and spake unto them, saying, "All power is given unto me in heaven and in earth" (Matt. 28:18). This Jesus is also the Captain of our salvation and the first-born of multitudes of born-again children of God. We have been made like Him in all ways, and are one with Him—for this reason He is not ashamed to call us brothers and sisters (Heb. 2:11-17).

While He was on the earth, Jesus suffered all the things that He did so that

> . . . he might be a merciful and faithful high priest in things pertaining to God, to make reconciliation for the sins of the people. For in that he himself hath suffered being tempted, he is able to succour them that are tempted (Heb. 2:17-18).

Because of this, the writer of Hebrews then tells us to hold *fast our profession* ("profession" means "confession" and refers to the things we say) because "we have a great high priest, that is passed into the heavens, Jesus the Son of God . . ." and ". . . not an high priest which cannot be touched with the feeling of our infirmities; but was in all points tempted like as we are, yet without sin" (Heb. 4:14-15).

This is important for us to understand. If Jesus had not been tempted in the same areas we are, He could not give us assistance and relief. We could not go to Him for the comfort, guidance and strength we so often need. He could not understand what we feel and the difficulties we go through. He could not relate to our struggles at all. He does understand, however, for He was tempted in every way that we are. Jesus suffered the same things we suffer. He felt what we feel, He was tempted like we are tempted, and He was tried like we are tried. He endured all this so that He could understand and relate to what we feel. By going through those things and defeating them for me, I can go through them and be an overcomer. What power this imparts to me! He who knew no sin became sin for us so that the righteousness of God would be manifested in us (2 Cor. 5:21).

In Hebrews 11, we find God's "Honor Roll of Faith," or the "Faith Hall of Fame." The chapter lists the godly men and women who overcame tough times by faith and all the wonderful things God did for and through them. Like Abraham, they believed God and it was counted unto them for righteousness (Rom. 4:3).

These patriarchs of faith are watching us as we face the tests and challenges of life. They are cheering us on: "Wherefore seeing we also are compassed about with so great a cloud of witnesses . . ." (Heb. 12:1). These warriors of faith are testimonies to how Christians who live by faith can overcome the worst circumstances that come into their lives.

GOD WANTS TO BUILD OUR FAITH

When you were saved, God gave you a seed-measure of faith (Rom. 12:3). It's all the faith you need, but it's in seed form. In the parable of the sower, Jesus taught

21

how spiritual seeds develop (Mark 4:1-20). No matter how good the seed, it will not grow and produce unless it's in the right ground. To grow, seeds need fertile soil.

We need to nurture and cultivate our seed of faith. We do this by hearing the Word of God; but hearing is not enough, we must do what the Word says to do.

Some people talk about being burdened for lost souls, but have never won anyone to Christ. Some say they love to pray, but never spend much time in prayer or get any of their prayers answered. Others talk about tithing and giving, but never give sacrificially. All of us need less talk and more action. We need to do what we say. We need faith-action instead of just faith-words.

Sometimes we are kept from acting by the weight of the burdens and sins we carry. The Scripture says, ". . . let us lay aside every weight and the sin which doth so easily beset us . . ." (Heb. 12:1). The greatest sin that besets us is the sin of discouragement, because discouragement is the thing that really stops us from getting an answer from God. We get discouraged; we grow weary and we faint. This is sin, and it may well be the root of most sins.

MISSING THE MARK

In Hebrews 12:1, the Greek word that is translated *sin* is *hamartia*. Harmartia means to miss the mark. Missing the mark has different meanings in a skill like archery. For skilled archers, to miss the bull's eye is to miss their mark. For unskilled or amateur archers, just to hit the target is to hit their mark. The difference in perspective depends on where you are in your pursuit of your goal and where you want to be.

The Lord said to me, "You know why many people don't develop their faith and go on in me? They have areas of weakness in which they miss the mark, and every time they miss the mark it discourages them."

Missing the mark can cause Christians to believe and confess, "I can't do it. I'm weak. I can't overcome." These areas of weakness can become strongholds of the devil in their lives. Furthermore, Satan will immediately add to their discouragement by telling them, "You've never been an overcomer, and you never will be one!"

The devil is a liar! The Apostle Paul said, "I can do all things through Christ which strengtheneth me" (Phil. 4:13). Christ himself, in all the power and glory of His resurrected life, dwells in you, and He said, "If ye abide in me, and my words abide in you, ye shall ask what ye will, and it shall be done unto you." It is our responsibility to *lay aside* every weight and sin, especially those sins that the devil keeps throwing in our faces. A woman once said to me, "The devil keeps bringing up my past. What should I do?"

I said to her, "When the devil brings up your past, bring up his past. Tell him how Jesus went down to hell, knocked his teeth out, took the keys to death and hell, stripped him of his authority and power, made a show of him openly, triumphed over him, rose from the dead, ascended to glory and sits on the right hand of power. Remind him that Jesus has clearly said to you, 'Behold I give you authority to tread on serpents and scorpions and all the power of the enemy and nothing shall by any means hurt you.' When the devil reminds you of your past, remind him of his past."

Sometimes our praying isn't effective because we're

discouraged and disheartened. We may pray, "God, I am so weak, please take this weight off my back." That prayer misses the mark because the Scriptures don't tell us to ask God to remove the weight from us, they command us to remove the weight ourselves—to lay it aside.

Let's do it. Let's lay it aside. There are things that God will do for us and there are things that He requires us to do. When the Scriptures tell us that *we* are to do something, we have to do those things for ourselves—God won't do them for us.

When we have been commanded to lay it aside, it's not appropriate to pray, "Lord, if you want to take this away from me, you can take it away." If the Word says that doing something is not God's will for you, then it is not God's responsibility to stop you from doing it—it's your responsibility. God has given you the power to accomplish His will in your life. He has given you power to become a son of God (John 1:12). You have the power to overcome the devil. You can lay aside the weight and sin that are holding you back from victory. Appropriate the power and the promise in the Scripture that says: " . . . let the weak say, I am strong" (Joel 3:10).

Instead of saying, "I'm weak," say, "In Christ, I'm strong!" Instead of saying, "I'm going under," start saying, "In Christ, I'm going over!" It's time for you to realize that Christ is in you and you are in Him—and "greater is he that is in you than he that is in the world."

Sometimes you ask someone how he is and he replies, "I'm doing well under the circumstances." I always want to say to him, "What are you doing under the circumstances?" Read Romans 8 every time you're tempted to say that. It's time we realized that we've been justified, sanctified and made righteous. We are a holy people. We are light and righteousness. Nothing can separate us from the love of God.

Sometimes, in order to lay aside the weights and sin that hamper our walk, we have to break fellowship with certain people. Misery loves company, and when this dynamic is operating in a relationship, we need to sever that relationship. It's almost as if some people have "the gift of discouragement."

There are people you can be around who will bring out the best in you But the opposite will also happen. I know certain people who bring out the worst in me, and I do my best to stay away from them. I need to be with optimistic faith people. Some people brighten the room when they enter it, others brighten the room when they leave it. God's people should be bright lights both entering and leaving.

PATIENT ENDURANCE

> Wherefore seeing we also are compassed about with so great a cloud of witnesses, let us lay aside every weight, and the sin which doth so easily beset us, and let us run with patience the race that is set before us, Looking unto Jesus the author and finisher of our faith . . . (Heb. 12:1-2).

Unless it's raining, I ride a bike every morning. While riding one morning, I was meditating on chapter twelve of Hebrews. As I meditated, the impor-tance of patient endurance was revealed to me. You don't get anywhere when you jump over territory you *must* cross. Life isn't a game of Monopoly™. You don't pass GO and collect $200. Life involves problems and adversities that we must endure to grow. So let's run our race of faith with patient endurance. A successful life requires traveling through each milestone, each place, each location. You don't develop a victorious, godly life by jumping over five squares of problems and adversities that you need to learn to overcome with God's help.

Keep your spiritual goals in front of you, otherwise you'll have no stimulus to continue. When in a race, we must know the course and where the goal is. If I know where I'm going and how to get there, I can endure the situations that confront me. I can endure the difficulty of biking up the last hill because I know that when I get to the top, I'll have a clear view of the rest of my journey. Before I get there, I may feel like I'll never make it and ask, "Where's the last hill? Where's the top?" But I always know that it's there, somewhere ahead of me, and that I'll make it if I endure.

The race of life is filled with hills that must be climbed and valleys that must be crossed. The Scriptures tell us how to run the race and how to win it: ". . . run with patience the race that is set before us, Looking unto Jesus the author and finisher of our faith . . ." (Heb. 12:1-2).

Jesus is our goal-setter. The goal-setter always goes before the runners. Jesus has already experienced what we experience. He has already felt what we feel. He has already been tempted like us. He experienced pain and depression for us, and felt lonely and rejected. But He overcame every step of the way, and now He is ready to make sure that we have everything we need to overcome, just as He overcame (Rev. 3:21).

Our answer is Jesus—He is "the author and finisher of our faith." The word "author" is better translated "originator," and the word "finisher" is better translated "perfecter." He is the originator and perfecter of our faith. The bottom line is that we cannot win the race without faith in Him.

In the race of life, we are to keep looking at Jesus, our goal-setter, because He is the originator and perfecter of faith! Faith finds its origination and perfection in Jesus, "who for the joy that was set before him endured the cross, despising the shame, and is set down at the right hand of the throne of God" (Heb. 12:2b). Jesus stayed in the will of God through the pain and degradation of the cross because there was a reward ahead of Him that would bring Him great joy.

We are to keep our eyes upon Jesus, the originator and perfecter of our faith, and have the same attitude that He did and run with patience the specific race of life that God has determined for each of us: "For consider him that endured such contradiction of sinners against himself, lest ye be wearied and faint in your minds" (Heb. 12:3).

LEARNING FROM JESUS' LIFE

Our Lord Jesus shows us how to cope when tough times come. He suffered in all the areas that we have or ever will suffer. Look at just these areas alone.

1. Jesus suffered rejection.

Every person on the earth has been rejected many times in their past, and will be many times before they die. Rejection is a part of life. It is an experience—never pleasant—that we all go through many times. Fortunately, as Christians we have a Lord and High Priest who went

27

through rejections for us, knows how painful they sometimes are, and can help and strengthen us. The Scripture tells us, "He came unto his own, and his own received him not" (John 1:11).

God created all things through His Son, then, after a passage of time, sent Him from His throne of glory to earth to reconcile all things to God. The ones the Son created, especially the chosen house of Israel, rejected Him and would not recognize Him as God's anointed One. Of Jesus, Isaiah wrote, "He is despised and rejected of men; a man of sorrows, and acquainted with grief . . ." (Isa. 53:3). When we're hurting from rejection, we need to look to the love and acceptance of our Lord for strength and peace, and to His life on the earth to teach us how to respond to those who rejected us. Though rejected, the Son of God kept on loving, praying and doing the work His Father sent Him to do. In His name, let us do the same.

2. Jesus suffered persecution.

Jesus experienced persecution of the worst sort. He came down from heaven to give people abundant life, yet they accused Him of being a liar and once tried to throw Him off a cliff. He healed people and set them free from bondage by casting out devils by the Spirit of God, yet they accused him of casting them out by Beelzebub, the Prince of Devils. He ate with the unrighteous to speak to them of the kingdom of God, and they called him ". . . a gluttonous man, and a winebibber, a friend of publicans and sinners!" (Luke 7:34). For over three years He ". . . went about doing good, and healing all that were oppressed of the devil . . ."

28

(Acts 10:38), and they hung Him on a Cross on Calvary.

It was from that Cross that Jesus looked down upon those who had nailed Him to it and said, "Father, forgive them for they know not what they do" (Luke 23:34). Our Lord loved His enemies, blessed them that cursed Him, did good to those that hated Him, and prayed for those that despitefully used Him and persecuted Him (Matt. 5:44). Let's take up our cross and follow His example— no matter where He leads us or how difficult it is.

3. Jesus was harassed by the devil.

Ever feel harassed by the devil? Read Luke 4 and Matthew 4 about how Jesus was tempted in the wilderness by Satan. We aren't told much about the daily temptations while Jesus fasted for forty days, but we are told about the worst temptations at the end of forty days when He was near starvation (that's the meaning of the KJV words, "was afterwards ahungered" or "afterward hungered"). Satan came to Him and said, "If thou be the Son of God, command this stone that it be made bread" (Luke 4:3). The devil isn't going to tempt you in an area in which you're not likely to fall.

Now if we were in that situation and the devil tempted us, we'd probably say, "Hey, that's right. I don't have to wait until I get to a restaurant, I've got the power." Then, with the devil's approval, we'd wave our hands over some rocks and make bread—and ruin our entire relationship with God. But not the Lord. He looked at the devil and said, "It is written, That man shall not live by bread alone, but by every word of God" (Luke 4:4). The devil could have tempted Jesus with every food in the world and it wouldn't have made any difference.

Nothing could make the Son of God disobey His Father.

So the devil, like he will always do, tried again. This time he took Jesus

> . . . up into an high mountain, shewed unto him all the kingdoms of the world in a moment of time. And the devil said unto him, All this power will I give thee, and the glory of them: for that is delivered unto me; and to whomsoever I will I give it. If thou therefore wilt worship me, all shall be thine (Luke 4:5-7).

In other words, you don't have to go through all your Father says you have to go through to gain back control of the world, just bow down to me and I'll turn the world over to you. Simple, painless, easy. But the Lord would have nothing to do with the devil, and said, ". . . Get thee behind me, Satan: for it is written, Thou shalt worship the Lord thy God, and him only shalt thou serve" (Luke 4:8).

Still the devil wouldn't give up. Sound familiar? He came at Jesus again "And brought him to Jerusalem, and set him on a pinnacle of the temple, and said unto him, If thou be the Son of God, cast thyself down from hence: For it is written, He shall give his angels charge over thee, to keep thee: and in their hands they shall bear thee up, lest at any time thou dash thy foot against a stone" (Luke 4:9-11).

This temptation would be like my saying, "You need to test your faith. So let's go to the top of the Empire State Building and you jump off. Psalm 91:11 says God '. . . shall give His angels charge over you.'" You'd be stupid to do it. And if I said it and you believed it, we should both be locked up. The laws of the State of New

York would be against me for telling you to do such a thing, and the law of gravity would be against you for doing it.

The devil said to Jesus, "Just throw yourself off. You're the Son of God. He will give His angels charge over you." Jesus responded by telling him, "It is said, Thou shalt not tempt the Lord thy God." (Luke 4:12). That ended the temptations, all of which proves that though the devil may keep at you for awhile, if you stand in faith he will eventually give up.

The devil is real and his attacks are real. He tempted Jesus, and you can be sure he will tempt you and try to attack you. At those times, don't be afraid—just remember that Jesus was like us and was anointed with the Holy Ghost, and His same power is in us.

The devil is always testing and persecuting God's people. You and I may think, even say, "I don't know why the devil is always at me; I love Jesus." That's precisely why he's always attacking us. Because he knows that the more we fall in love with Jesus, the greater threat we are to him.

When tough times—tests, trials and temptations—come your way, remember that Jesus faced them before you did. His life and power within you will enable you to face them and conquer them. He'll strengthen you within your spirit, and you'll be able to stand in faith. When that happens, do what Jesus did—speak God's Word to the devil and watch him flee from you.

> There hath no temptation has taken you but such as is common to man: but God is faithful, who will not suffer [permit] you to be tempted above that ye are able; but will with the temptation also make a way of escape, that ye may be able to bear it (1 Cor. 10:13).

31

3

Push On Through

God wants a people who are strong and determined—a people who won't be intimidated by trials and difficulties that come against them and who will push through those adversities to victory. If we want to be those people, the first thing we must learn is that,

> There hath no temptation taken you but such as is common to man: but God is faithful, who will not suffer you to be tempted above that ye are able; but will with the temptation also make a way to escape, that ye may be able to bear it (1 Cor. 10:13).

In other words, no matter how difficult your problem, you aren't the only one who ever had to face it, and God has made a way for you to escape. He has provided a way out of every temptation. God is faithful. He will not allow more to come against you than you can stand. He will make a way for you so "that ye may be able to bear it," which means you'll be able to handle it without falling apart or ruining everything.

God wants us to know that He is ". . . a very present help in trouble" (Ps. 46:1), and that He is always doing for us what He said He would do. The fact that you have problems and that there sometimes appears to be a delay in His answer doesn't change the fact that He's working on your behalf. All too often our attitude about His answering us is like that of the person who prayed for patience: "God, I want patience and I want it now!"

Many of those in the Bible had to go through tough times. Jesus warned Peter, ". . . Satan hath desired to have you, that he may sift you as wheat: But I have prayed for thee that thy faith fail not: and when thou art converted, strengthen thy brethren." (Luke 22:31-32). Jesus said He had prayed for Peter's faith not to fail. He didn't say He had prayed to get Peter out of the testing. In other words, He was telling Peter, "You'll have to stand by faith in Me and my Words. You'll have to fight the devil and push him back. I've given you the power to do it, and I won't do it for you." As we said before, don't be praying to God to get the devil off your back when you've been given the power to do it. So start resisting Satan and get him away from you!

In the previous chapter, we listed three adversities in Jesus' life: 1. He was rejected; 2. He was persecuted; 3. He was harassed by the devil. It was by pushing through these things He suffered that He learned obedience (Heb. 5:8), and this is how we learn obedience. There is not a different way for us than there was for Jesus. We need to walk in our Master's footsteps as we face life's tough times. Now let's add to our list four more adversities in Jesus' life and see how He pushed through them.

4. They wanted to kill Jesus.

Once Jesus asked those who did not believe in Him, ". . . Why go ye about to kill me?" (John 7:19). But the answer He already knew—it was because He was preaching what they did not want to hear. Sometimes, the greatest threat to the Gospel of Jesus Christ is religious people. Their doctrine often blinds them to the truths that are in God's Word. As a result, such people often are in bondage to lies.

Jesus came and preached to a religious system that did not like Him. They did not want to change because they were in a comfortable position. They didn't see their real needs and they certainly didn't want their comfort zone encroached upon by anyone. In fact, the truth that Jesus was preaching so upset them that they had to find a reason to reject it, so they answered Him ". . . and said, Thou hast a devil: who goeth about to kill thee? (John 7:20).

Can you imagine such a response to Jesus? These religious people accused the Son of God of having a devil—and then pretended they hadn't tried to do anything to Him by saying, "who goeth about to kill thee?" Jesus' only answer to them was, "Judge not according to the appearance, but judge righteous judgment" (John 7:24). That's a good answer for us to remember.

5. Jesus' credentials were questioned.

Jesus said about himself:

> . . . I am the light of the world: he that followeth me shall not walk in darkness, but shall have the light of life. The Pharisees therefore said unto him, Thou

bearest record of thyself; thy record is not true. Jesus answered and said unto them, Though I bear record of myself, yet my record is true: for I know whence I came, and whither I go; but ye cannot tell whence I come, and whither I go. Ye judge after the flesh; I judge no man. And yet if I judge, my judgment is true: for I am not alone, but I and the Father that sent me. It is also written in your law, that the testimony of two men is true. I am one that bear witness of myself, and the Father that sent me beareth witness of me (John 8:12-18).

The Pharisees would not accept Jesus' testimony about himself—His spiritual credentials—and they never did have faith in His integrity, so "Then said they unto him, Where is thy Father?" Jesus didn't reply directly to their question—which was His usual way of handling questions—but ". . . answered, Ye neither know me, nor my Father: if ye had known me, ye should have known my Father also." (John 8:19). Jesus said these things in the Pharisees' stronghold and source of income, the treasure in the temple, and it apparently made them so mad that they tried to physically hurt Him, because the Scripture says, ". . . and no man laid hands on him; for his hour was not yet come" (John 8:20).

They wanted to get hold of Jesus, but weren't able to. They were prevented from being able to do that, "for His hour had not yet come, so they kept questioning Him: "Where do you come from?" "Where are you going?" "What right do you have to tell us these things? Who sent you?" They wouldn't stop, but kept right after Him.

Now, rather than letting up and making things easier on them, and easier in every way on himself, as we would probably do, Jesus increased the spiritual pressure on them—and, remember, He said all this in Solomon's Temple, the center of Israel's religious beliefs and life.

> . . . If I honour myself, my honour is nothing: it is my Father that honoureth me; of whom ye say, that he is your God: Yet ye have not known him; but I know him: and if I should say, I know him not, I shall be a liar like unto you: but I know him, and keep his saying. Your father Abraham rejoiced to see my day: and he saw it, and was glad (John 8:54-56).

You can understand how that last statement must have really burned these religious leaders—it went right against many of their most cherished beliefs and teachings, and they came back at Him and said, ". . . Thou art not yet fifty years old, and hast thou seen Abraham?" (John 8:57). (It's interesting that Jesus was actually only about thirty-three years old, but apparently He looked like He was close to fifty, which should give us an idea of the kind of life He had.)

Again, instead of making it easy on them and on himself, Jesus increased the spiritual and mental pressure on them—and the pressure on their interpretation of the Scriptures about the Messiah who was to come—and said to them, ". . . Verily, verily, I say unto you, Before Abraham was, I am." (John 8:58)

The religious leaders and their followers had had enough of this upstart, this false prophet who claimed that God was His Father and that He had existed even before their father Abraham, whom He said was glad to see His day—so, "Then took they up stones to cast at him . . . " (John 8:59).

But it didn't do them any good. They could not take

hold of Jesus and they could not stone Him, because His time had not yet come, so ". . . Jesus hid himself, and went out of the temple, going through the midst of them, and so passed by" (John 8:59). This is something we always want to remember in our lives—nothing can touch us except in God's time and for God's purpose and glory and to do us good (Rom. 8:28).

We may get intimidated and upset when people come against us and treat us wrongly when we have done nothing wrong. When this happens, we need to remember that people also came against Jesus—a man who went around doing nothing but good. And if someone challenges our faith or our proclaiming of Christ as Lord and Savior and the only Way to God, it's time to be strong in faith instead of weak in fear. "For God hath not given us the spirit of fear; but of power, and of love, and of a sound mind" (2 Tim. 1:7). We must *never* be ashamed of the Gospel of Jesus Christ, for it is the power of God unto salvation.

6. Jesus' right to do the work of God was challenged.

In John 9, we read how Jesus healed the man who was blind from birth. The disciples came to Him and asked, ". . . Master, who did sin, this man, or his parents, that he was born blind?" (John 9:2) These are the Sons of Thunder—James and John—who are asking this question. They're men of faith!

> Jesus answered: Neither hath this man sinned, nor his parents: but that the works of God should be made manifest in him. I must work the works of him that sent me, while it is day: the night cometh, when no man can work (John 9:3-4).

In effect, Jesus said, "We're not going to worry about why it happened. I'm going to work the works of Him who sent me and heal the blind man. Forget about how or why it happened. I'M GOING TO HEAL HIM!"

> When he had thus spoken, he spat on the ground, and made clay of the spittle, and he anointed the eyes of the blind man with the clay, And said unto him, Go, wash in the pool of Siloam, (which is by interpretation, Sent.) He went his way therefore, and washed, and came seeing (John 9:6-7).

Some people who had heard about the miracle and knew the man, asked him, "What happened? Who did this?"

The man replied, "A man called Jesus put clay upon my eyes and told me to go to the pool of Siloam and wash. And I went and washed and I received sight."

They asked, "Where is He?"

"I don't know," the man replied. He wasn't trying to find out where Jesus was at this point. He was immersed in happiness over the gift of eyesight.

So the people did what all good religious people do in the face of a miracle they can't understand: "They brought to the Pharisees him that aforetime was blind. And it was the sabbath day when Jesus made the clay, and opened his eyes" (John 9:13-14).

I believe Jesus did certain things, like healing on the Sabbath, just to stir up the religious leaders and get them thinking about their religious doctrines, and perhaps show some of their followers how foolish their doctrines were.

> Then again the Pharisees also asked him how he had received his sight. He said unto them, He put clay upon mine eyes, and I washed, and do see. Therefore said some of the Pharisees, This man is not of God . . . (John 9:15-16).

A blind man who had been blind since birth could now see, and these religious leaders said that Jesus was not of God! Where was their logic? What kind of logic was it? Here is a sampling: ". . . because he keepeth not the sabbath day. Others said, How can a man that is a sinner do such miracles . . . ?" (John 9:16).

They judged Jesus to be not of God, and thus a sinner, because He performed this healing on the Sabbath. In those days, you were not permitted to work on the Sabbath. Jesus had an answer for their doctrine of bondage: ". . . Which of you shall have an ass or an ox fallen into a pit, and will not straightway pull him out on the sabbath day?" (Luke 14:5). Jesus was pointing to the double-mindedness that exists in the heart of man. Most of us have two sets of rules—one for us and one for everybody else. This was true of the religious leaders in Jesus' time—and some Christians today.

Most of us "get all bent out of shape" if someone challenges our credibility like the Pharisees did Jesus'. It's upsetting in many ways. It may even cause us to doubt ourselves. We may even want to run and hide, or run to church to complain—or be pitied. It's time for us to stop being intimidated when we're challenged. It's true that there are a lot of sinners in the world who will come at us, and a lot of Christians in the Church who will do the same; but God is on our side. Our trouble is that we often don't consider His greatness or His work on our behalf. We look at the situations and circumstances instead of God, who is greater than anything or anyone that can come against us.

7. Jesus felt sorrow, grief and loneliness.
The prophet Isaiah wrote,

> He is despised and rejected of men; a man of sorrows, and acquainted with grief: and we hid as it were our faces from him; he was despised, and we esteemed him not (Isa. 53:3).

Thinking of what Jesus was like, we might be tempted to say, "No. Not my Master. Not my Savior." But it is recorded in Matthew 26 and Luke 22 that when Jesus went to the Garden of Gethsemane to pray, He asked His disciples to watch and pray while He went further into the garden to be alone with His Father. Luke says that His agony was so great that bloody sweat dropped from Him (Luke 22:44). Yet when He went back to His disciples in that terrible hour, He found them "asleep, and saith unto Peter, What, could ye not watch with me one hour?" (Matt. 26:40). Also, it was only a little while later that all His disciples deserted Him when the soldiers came, He was alone during His torture and trial, and almost none of them were at His Cross. He had ministered to thousands.

As a faith-person, there are times when you'll feel alone, rejected and challenged. There are times when your credentials and credibility will be questioned. Don't think you're going to walk in the Spirit without these things happening to you. You'll be rejected, harassed, and persecuted by the devil and those he uses. The important thing is how you'll respond to each trial.

Jesus said,

> These things I have spoken unto you, that in me
> ye might have peace. In the world ye shall have
> tribulation: but be of good cheer; I have overcome the
> world (John 16:33).

If we hold onto this truth, we'll be able to deal with the tough times in the same way Jesus did.

When I face spiritual trials, I know it means my life is where it should be. When I'm not challenged, it means my life's in a neutral state. The devil never challenges Christians who are driving in neutral. He only challenges Christians who are in "Drive!" Pastor Buddy Harrison said, "Two-thirds of God's name is Go." When we're moving with God, opposition will come—or rather, we'll run into it where it is. Demonic forces are threatened by our life of faith; so let's threaten them all we can and hit them head on. As faith-people, we're not driving Volkswagens, but tanks!

NEHEMIAH AND TOUGH TIMES

Nehemiah exemplifies how a tough person responds to tough times with the help of our good God. Nehemiah was a cupbearer to the king, and somebody whom God found was willing to do something that other people were apparently unwilling to do.

Nehemiah was disturbed when he heard that the walls of Jerusalem had been broken down. When God's people hear about a need, God wants them to do something about it. God has called us to be people with solutions, not problems. Like Nehemiah, the first thing we should do is pray and ask the Lord to help us.

> O Lord, I beseech thee, let now thine ear be attentive to the prayer of thy servant, and to the prayer of thy servants, who desire to fear thy name: and prosper, I pray thee, thy servant this day, and grant him mercy in the sight of this man. For I was the king's cupbearer (Neh. 1:11).

Soon after, while he was serving the king, the king saw that he was sad and asked him what was wrong. Nehemiah told him and asked the king's permission to go to Jerusalem in order to repair the walls. The king agreed. When Nehemiah got to Judah, God provided him with people to help him. When you're walking in God's will and doing work that you can't do alone, God will always provide you with help. Count on Him for it.

THE GOOD HAND OF GOD UPON US

Nehemiah requested several things from the king, and the king granted them all. Nehemiah tells why he did: ". . . And the king granted me, according to the good hand of my God upon me" (Neh. 2:8). When the hand of God is on you, it doesn't matter what God wants you to do, or what people think about your qualifications. God's hand on you will even make people favor you who don't want to favor you.

Nehemiah went to Jerusalem and got the people together even though he knew they did not understand why he was there. He wasn't their choice, and they hadn't sent for him. You may not be not the people's choice, or even called by them, but if you are God's choice, it is the only credential you need to accomplish His work. If God is for you, who can be against you? (Rom. 8:31).

After Nehemiah viewed the wall at Jerusalem, he went back to those who had gathered with him and—in his own words, ". . . told them of the hand of my God which was good upon me; as also the king's words that he had spoken unto me . . ." (Neh. 2:18).

Nehemiah was absolutely certain that God was with him. He keep repeating his conviction and shared it with the people who came to work with him. When he did, "they said, Let us rise up and build." And Nehemiah says, ". . . So they strengthened their hands for this good work" (Neh. 2:18). When you're convinced that the hand of God is on you, and others who hear your testimony become convinced too, you'll have willing people to help you do the work God has given you to do.

Don't think, however, that just because the people decided to help Nehemiah that the devil was going to leave them alone. Never think that way. Just because it's God who gives you something to do, doesn't mean the devil will stay away. Quite the contrary, he'll always try to defeat God's work.

When the people said they would rise up to work, Nehemiah said to them, ". . . The God of heaven, he will prosper us; therefore we his servants will arise and build . . ." (Neh. 2:20). With these words he was assuring them that God would bless their efforts. In other words, he said, "You look to me as your leader and that's fine, but it's not my ability, or my strength, or my knowledge that counts. All that counts is that God is with me and has told me what to do." We need to distinguish between natural ability and divine ability. It's the anointing of the Holy Ghost that breaks the yoke of bondage and sets people and things free for the work of God.

Two Kinds of Workers

Nehemiah then writes about all the repairs the wall needed and about the opposition they faced:

> But it came to pass, that when Sanballat heard that we builded the wall, he was wroth, and took great indignation, and mocked the Jews. And he spake before his brethren and the army of Samaria, and said, What do these feeble Jews? will they fortify themselves? will they sacrifice? will they make an end in a day? will they revive the stones out of the heaps of the rubbish which are burned? Now Tobiah the Ammonite was by him, and he said, Even that which they build, if a fox go up, he shall even break down their stone wall (Neh. 4:1-3).

Then when these scoffers ". . . heard that the walls of Jerusalem were made up, and that the breaches began to be stopped, then they were very wroth," (Neh. 4:7), and they ". . . conspired all of them together to come and to fight against Jerusalem, and to hinder it" (Neh. 4:8).

What Nehemiah did then is a good lesson for all of us who are doing God's work and have the enemy and his people come against us: "We made our prayer unto our God, and set a watch against them day and night, (Neh. 4:9). What happened as a result of prayer and preparation? Listen to Nehemiah again, "And it came to pass, when our enemies heard that it was known unto us, and God had brought their counsel to nought, that we returned all of us to the wall, every one unto his work" (Neh. 4:15).

Not a bad formula for protecting and maintaining God's work! When you sense the enemy coming against the work, do three things: 1, pray; 2, prepare for battle and watch for the enemy; 3, return to the work. Remember, the battle is the Lord's. When opposition comes, stand fast, set yourself, and expect to see God's mighty deliverance.

Worry and anxiety about the enemy's attack is never the appropriate response. Our concern should not relate to what is coming against us from the outside—the reproach, the criticism, the anger, the insults—for God will take care of that. We do, however, need to watch for the rubbish that accumulates where we're building, and we need to make sure to clean out the rubbish wherever we are. The world outside our church is not going to stop us, but we can be stopped from problems inside our church. A house divided against itself shall not stand (Matt. 12:25).

Nehemiah assigned half the people to be builders and half to be watchers—watchmen on the wall. The watchmen are the intercessors. Every church needs intercessors on its spiritual walls who are watching and praying not only for the church leaders and workers, but for all the members of the church. "Praying always with all prayer and supplication in the Spirit, and watching thereunto with all perseverance and supplication for all saints" (Eph. 6:18).

For though we walk in the flesh, we do not war after the flesh: (For the weapons of our warfare are not carnal, but mighty through God to the pulling down of strongholds) . . . (2 Cor. 10:3-4).

Both kinds of workers are needed: workers to build walls, workers to watch and fight spiritual battles and pull down strongholds.

Let's each seek God to find out which kind of worker He has made us. Once He has told us, and we are confident in what He has said, then let us be about our Father's business, and push through until it's completed to His glory.

4

The Danger of Discouragement

Deep discouragement will take you out of the things of God. We must constantly guard ourselves against the enemy of discouragement. Even strong people get discouraged when they face adversities. Some of us think that because we have faith we're never going to have problems. God didn't give you the shield of faith to display on your wall—it's to use for protection when you face problems.

THE REAL WAR

God gave us His weapons of warfare because there's a real war going on around us, and the enemy's not using rubber bullets. The devil's a real enemy and his goal is to destroy every Christian. If he can, he'll discourage us and try to make us feel like we're not worthy to be a child of God.

A sense of unworthiness has defeated many sincere souls. People will say, "I'm not worthy. I'm just an old sinner." It's true that you *were* no good, but you're not that way anymore. The blood of Jesus washed you clean and you're now the righteousness of God, and the Holy Ghost lives inside of you. God's working in you to make you perfect, and He's given you a Name to use that is above every name.

Many discouraging situations will come your way. The question is: "How long will you stay discouraged?" The closer you get to God, the more the enemy will try to discourage you. But the closer you get to God, the stronger you'll get as the light of His glory shines on you and floods you.

Notice what happened to the Israelites as they got closer to the Promised Land:

> . . . the soul of the people was much discouraged because of the way. And the people spake against God, and against Moses, Wherefore have ye brought us up out of Egypt to die in the wilderness? for there is no bread, neither is there any water; and our soul loatheth this light bread [manna]. And the LORD sent fiery serpents among the people, and they bit the people; and much people of Israel died. Therefore the people came to Moses, and said, We have sinned, for we have spoken against the LORD, and against thee; pray unto the LORD, that he take away the serpents from us. And Moses prayed for the people. And the LORD said unto Moses, Make thee a fiery serpent, and set it upon a pole: and it shall come to pass, that every one that is bitten, when he looketh upon it, shall live. And Moses made a serpent of brass, and put it upon a pole, and it came to pass, that if a serpent had bitten any man, when he beheld the serpent of brass, he lived (Num. 21:4-9).

See how people can get their eyes off God? If you look into the history of these people, you'll find that God blessed and protected them time and again. He was constantly watching over them. But we see by their example how quickly people forget from where God had brought them, how He had blessed them, and how He had been with them every step of the way. We always seem to accentuate the negative. Too many Christians are always negative, always complaining. We need to remember the good things God has done in our lives. When we learn to count our blessings, we'll be amazed at all that God has done for us!

The first three verses of Numbers 21 tell us how the people praised God for giving them a victory. But, as ". . . they journeyed from mount Hor by the way of the Red sea, to compass the land of Edom: and the soul of the people was much discouraged because of the way" (Num. 21:4). The Amplified Bible (AMP) expands that passage to say, "and the people became impatient (depressed, much discouraged) because [of the trials] of the way."

Discouragement takes over when you take your eyes off God and start looking at your situations and circumstances—like your physical, spiritual, social, or financial needs. Many Christians today are like the Israelites—discouraged and depressed. They've lost their patience because what they wanted to happen hasn't yet happened, and they've started to doubt God. Why would any Christian do that?

As His children, we're supposed to learn and understand our Father's ways. If He split the Red Sea for the Israelites, sent them manna from heaven, caused the east wind to blow and bring them quail, and defeated their enemies every time, He'll surely bless us in similar ways. His Word assures us that He is the same yesterday, today and forever. Never lose your perspective of God when tough times come. Keep in mind what Paul said: "Being confident of this very thing, that he which hath begun a good work in you will perform it until the day of Jesus Christ" (Phil. 1:6).

KEEP YOUR EYES ON JESUS

The Israelites lost patience and were dispirited and depressed because of the trials that came their way. So naturally the first thing they did was start complaining about God and Moses. "God must have forsaken us. Why did you bring us out here? You brought us here to die."

When you hear Christians complaining and bad-mouthing other believers and church leaders, you can be certain they've taken their eyes off Jesus and wandered from their faith. If you're not on the path of faith, you're not on the Christian journey. The problem is that too many of us think that being comfortable equals living a successful life of faith.

What makes you feel comfortable in your Christian walk? If you say, "Oh, God is really blessing me right now, the devil hasn't bothered me for six months," then you probably haven't done anything for God in six months. We tend to think that when nothing is coming against us, God is blessing us. Wrong! If you're in a place where nothing is coming against you, it's probably because you've done nothing to worry the devil.

Losing faith in God's Word is occurring with frightening regularity in the Church today. Many Christians have lost their joy because they've looked away from God and focused on the violent people, dangerous circumstances, and tragic conditions prevalent in the world today. Until you're absolutely focused on the Lord, you'll never have joy or strength and power in your life. Remember, ". . . the joy of the Lord is your strength" (Neh. 8:10). It's *His* joy that gives you strength.

When the Israelites in the wilderness spoke against God and Moses, ". . . the LORD sent fiery serpents among the people, and they bit the people; and much people of Israel died" (Num. 21:6). They gave in to the sin of discouragement that places circumstances above God. Anytime we put something ahead of God, we sin. The greatest commandment of all says to, ". . . love the Lord thy God with all thy heart, and with all thy soul, and with all thy mind, and with all thy strength . . ." (Mark 12:30).

When the Israelites began to die, they stopped complaining about God and Moses and ran to Moses for help. "Therefore the people came to Moses, and said, We have sinned, for we have spoken against the LORD, and against thee; pray unto the LORD, that he take away the serpents from us. And Moses prayed for the people" (Num. 21:7). We'll often find this happening in our lives: people will talk against us until they need somebody to pray for them. When they do, we need to forget that they bad-mouthed us and pray for them like Moses did for the Israelites. Moses prayed, and the Lord told him to, ". . . Make thee a fiery serpent, and set it upon a pole: and it shall come to pass, that every one that is bitten, when he looketh upon it, shall live" (Num. 21:8). The pole, of course, symbolized the Cross, and the fiery serpent symbolized Christ. Remember what Jesus said to Nicodemus: ". . . As Moses lifted up the serpent in the wilderness, even so must the Son of man be lifted up . . ." (John 3:14).

Jesus was symbolized prophetically as the serpent on the pole. Why? Because He became sin for us. He gathered up every evil thing that human beings can conceive and took them to the Cross. Looking upon the One hanging on that Cross means salvation in the same way that looking upon the brass serpent on the pole saved the Israelites from death. This is a type of Christ in the Old Testament. As we behold Him, we live (Num. 21:9).

We become discouraged when in our eyes our problem becomes bigger than God. There have been tough times in the past when I actually found myself praying, "God, if you are there . . . ." How could I possibly start a prayer that way after all He's done for me? If we give any room to discouragement, we may even justify scolding God as we pray, "Lord, you know I love you; now how long are you going to leave me in this mess I got myself into?" God is so patient and merciful with us.

ALL-SUFFICIENT GRACE

More than half of the New Testament was written by the Apostle Paul. When I look at the life of the Apostle Paul, I look at a man who had plenty of human reasons to get discouraged. In his two epistles to the

Corinthians, he tells about many of the challenges he faced.

One thing almost everyone did was challenge his calling as an apostle. Notice the way he confirms his apostleship in the opening of almost all his epistles: "Paul, called to be an apostle of Jesus Christ through the will of God . . ." (1 Cor. 1:1). "Paul, an apostle of Jesus Christ by the will of God . . ." (2 Cor. 1:1, Eph. 1:1, Col. 1:1).

God used Paul to birth the church at Corinth, and now there were those who were telling the Corinthian Christians that Paul wasn't an apostle at all, that he did not have the credentials of an apostle (see Acts 1:21-22), and that "his letters, . . . are weighty and powerful; but his bodily presence is weak, and his speech contemptible" (2 Cor. 10:10). About this, Paul tells the Corinthians:

> But I fear, lest by any means, as the serpent beguiled Eve through his subtilty, so your minds should be corrupted from the simplicity that is in Christ. For if he that cometh preacheth another Jesus, whom we have not preached, or if ye receive another spirit, which ye have not received, or another gospel, which ye have not accepted, ye might well bear with him. For I suppose I was not a whit behind the very chiefest apostles. But though I be rude in speech, yet not in knowledge; but we have been throughly made manifest among you in all things (2 Cor. 11:3-6).

In other words, other preachers who claim to be somebody come to you and preach a different Jesus and another gospel and have a wrong spirit, and you listen to them and forget what I taught you. But I wasn't behind even the chiefest apostles in coming to you in power (1 Cor. 2:1-5), and in knowledge—even if my speech is rude.

Then Paul used their questioning of him to list his spiritual background, calling by God, and the marks of Christ on him—his battle-field credentials as an apostle:

> Are they Hebrews? So am I. Are they Israelites? so am I. Are they the seed of Abraham? so am I. Are they ministers of Christ? (I speak as a fool) I am more; in labours more abundant, in stripes above measure, in prisons more frequent, in deaths oft [at the point of death often]. Of the Jews five times received I forty stripes save one. Thrice was I beaten with rods, once was I stoned, thrice I suffered shipwreck, a night and a day I have been in the deep; in journeyings often, in perils of waters, in perils of robbers, in perils by mine own countrymen, in perils by the heathen, in perils in the city, in perils in the wilderness, in perils in the sea, in perils among false brethren; in weariness and painfulness, in watchings often, in hunger and thirst, in fastings often, in cold and nakedness. Beside those things that are without, that which cometh upon me daily, the care of all the churches. Who is weak, and I am not weak? Who is offended, and I burn not? If I must needs glory, I will glory of the things which concern mine infirmities (2 Cor. 11:22-30).

Paul could have complained, but he went on (in chapter 12) to speak of one—himself—who was lifted up into the third heaven: "Of such an one will I glory: yet of myself I will not glory, but in mine infirmities" (2 Cor. 12:5).

Paul did not say he would glory *because of* his

infirmities, but *in* them. This is a model for us to follow. When infirmities, tests and temptations come, they do not come from God. But when they do come, God will get glory out of them. That little word *"in"* blesses me, because it tells me that God can get glory out of my problems. The rest of this passage shows how Paul's infirmities happened:

> For though I would desire to glory, I shall not be a fool; for I will say the truth: but now I forbear, lest any man should think of me above that which he seeth me to be, or that he heareth of me. And lest I should be exalted above measure through the abundance of the revelations, there was given to me a thorn in the flesh, the messenger of Satan to buffet me, lest I should be exalted above measure (2 Cor. 12:6-7).

The word messenger is the same word translated "angel." This angel was not a godly angel; it was a demonic angel. Everywhere Paul went, Satan sent this angel to buffet him.

Paul then goes on to describe what this "thorn" was like. He had to be taken out of a city and put over a wall in a basket to escape to safety. Everywhere he went, he was harassed by demon spirits to stop the ministry of the Word. He was put in prison. He was beaten, stoned, shipwrecked—these circumstances all worked together to form the thorn in the flesh that Satan sent to keep God from exalting him.

The Bible says that if we humble ourselves, God will exalt us. Some people say, "I'm nothing. I'm just a nobody. I am just a poor . . . ." No, no, no—you *are* something! You are special in the eyes of God. "Humble yourselves therefore under the mighty hand of God, that he may exalt you in due time" (1 Pet. 5:6).

Paul was saying, in effect, "Satan is buffeting me, coming against me, because he knows the revelation I have of this whole New Testament of Jesus Christ." The disciples spent more than three years with Jesus and they did not have the revelation Paul had, and Paul never saw Him in the flesh. Then Paul said, "For this thing I besought the Lord thrice that it might depart from me" (2 Cor. 12:8). He was getting discouraged about it.

Did you ever wish some things weren't in the Scriptures? The reason we sometimes do is because we know that once we read them, we are responsible for doing them. The Lord said to Paul, ". . . My grace is sufficient for thee: for my strength is made perfect in weakness . . . (2 Cor. 12:9). (Note that the Lord didn't say, "My strength is made perfect through the anointing.") Once the Lord told Paul about His grace, Paul was responsible for learning to walk in it.

The Lord is giving an important principle here. He's telling Paul—and us—that if we learn to trust and depend on Him in the place of discouragement, even when we don't understand what's happening or why, His grace will always be sufficient for us. What a difference it would make to us in tough times if we would understand and learn this. By His grace, we can overcome *anything* the devil will put across our paths!

Faith-people want to know everything. We want to know why things happen the way they do, and we often ask the Lord to tell us. In some ways that good; in other ways it hurts our faith-walk. Instead of asking why, most of the time we need to ask what should I do now, what should I pray for, what steps should I take?

There will be plenty of tough times in life, but during those times, tough people dig into God and say, "God, I can't make it on my own. I don't have the strength or the fortitude. I feel discouraged; I feel weary and I am fainting in my mind. By my own wisdom and knowledge, I don't know where to turn, so *my eyes are on you and I'm trusting you.*"

Now we can better understand Paul's response:

> Most gladly therefore will I rather glory in my infirmities, that the power of Christ may rest upon me. Therefore I take pleasure in infirmities, in reproaches, in necessities, in persecutions, in distresses for Christ's sake: for when I am weak, then am I strong (2 Cor. 12:9-10).

Paul's not saying, "Bring on all the problems." What he's saying is something like, "I'm learning in these problems, in these distresses, in these persecutions, how to depend on my Lord. By His strength, when I'm weak and I can't make it, I grasp hold of His strength and His strength pulls me though my human weaknesses."

RISKS

Some things about our relationship with God are risky. I have heard some people teach that faith is not a risk. That's simply not true. The faith itself is not a risk because God gives it and honors it. However, each person has to activate his or her faith, has to personally get out of the boat and step onto the water; this involves a measure of risk. Don't tell me that when Peter put his foot on the water, it wasn't risky for him to do so. Unlike Peter, however, if we keep our eyes on the Lord and the all-sufficiency of His grace, we won't sink but will make it to where we're going. Even if we do sink a bit, the Lord will catch us and pull us back onto the surface.

SOWING AND REAPING

The Bible says, "Whatsoever a man soweth, that shall he also reap" (Gal. 6:7). People who sow sin reap the harvest of sin. People who are critical of others reap criticism to themselves. People who never sow love never reap love. People who never sow concern for others never reap concern from others. If you plant bitterness, anger, and discord, guess what you're going to get back? It's not love, joy, and peace. You're going to reap discord, anger, bitterness, and *lots* of strife.

Too many of us allow discouragement to get us down and love to have pity parties—for some, they're better than birthdays. When this happens we may say, "I'm going to leave this church. The people here don't love me or care about me." But if God plants you in a church pew, or in the choir, or in a position of leadership, you need to remain faithful to that calling by relying on His grace even when things get tough. Cultivate the good seeds that God has sown in you and in the Body of Christ. They will grow when you nurture and cultivate them. Remember, God's grace is *always* sufficient for you.

COUNTING IT ALL JOY

Paul was in Militus and he called for the elder of Ephesus, located just north of Militus. When they came to him, he said to them, "And now, behold, I go bound in the spirit unto Jerusalem, not knowing the things that shall befall me there: Save that the Holy Ghost witnesseth in every city, saying that bonds and afflictions abide me" (Acts 20:22-23).

Paul's next statement, which shows his response to this knowledge that the Holy Ghost has given him, shows how tough people ought to respond in tough times—and the reason why they should: "But none of these things move me, neither count I my life dear unto myself, so that I might finish my course with joy, and the ministry, which I have received of the Lord Jesus, to testify the gospel of the grace of God" (Acts 20:24).

Paul knew that allowing tough times to move him from his course for Christ would affect his joy—and his ministry for the Lord Jesus. He counted that joy as most important. When you seem to lose your joy and have replaced it with discouragement, do you know why you don't want to be in church? Because you don't want to be around when God is talking. He's liable to talk to you about being tough and standing fast in faith and keeping your joy. Remember what Jerry Savelle says, "If Satan can't steal your joy, he can't steal your goods."

God will restore your joy if you've been through tough times. He'll bring your joy back to you. The Apostle Paul said, in essence, "I am not moved by these things. I don't count my life dear to the death. I want to finish my course with joy. I'm not going to allow circumstances or those who want to kill, imprison and talk about me to bring me down and steal my joy. I'm not going to allow strife, prison, or people take me away from what God has called me to do. I'm going to keep

61

my eyes on Jesus." This is the mindset that always touches the Source of all joy.

Paul affirmed his approach to life in his epistle to the Philippians when he said, "I press toward the mark for the prize of the high calling of God in Christ Jesus" (Phil. 3:14). Tough times bring tough people to the forefront. I don't know of a tougher Christian than the Apostle Paul.

Tough times never discourage tough people—tough times strengthen them.

We grow in faith and conviction as a result of tough times.

Tough times can be overcome by tough people because of the grace of our good God!

5

Making Choices

When you know who you are in God, you don't have to be intimidated by anything or anybody the devil sends your way. He will use many people, even family and friends—both believers and unbelievers. Some of your worst problems will come from the "unbelieving believers," the doubting Thomases, the covenant people who don't know their covenant rights. They'll give you the most trouble. They'll try to talk you out of your faith. You'll say, "I'm believing God for this," and they'll say, "I tried that and it didn't work." They'll try to talk you out of your confidence, your healing, your financial blessing, and everything else God gave you.

When this happens, you're going to have to make some choices about Christian friends. One of the worst things is to choose Christian friends who don't have a heart after God. You need friends who encourage your faith, not tear it down. You need to be around people who strengthen you by their words—people who edify you and lift you up when you're down. Don't choose for a friend someone who will pamper you, but somebody who will tell you, "Get up! Start over again!"

If someone begins to criticize what you're believing about God's promises, tell him, "The Bible says: 'Greater is he that is in me than he that is in the world.' The Bible says, 'If God be for us, who can be against us?' The Bible says, 'And this is the victory that overcometh the world, even our faith.' The Bible says, 'For all the promises of God in him are yea, and in him Amen, unto the glory of God by us.'"

We have a right to say what the Bible says. Our doctrine should always come out of the epistles, which tell us in whom, by whom, of whom and through whom we shall prevail. Because of our oneness with Christ, we can declare, "Who He is, we are. As He is, so are we in this world."

As faith people, we may have misled some people over the years. Too many get saved and, when a trial comes their way, they complain, "I never knew this was going to happen. I thought that after I got saved nothing like this would ever happen again." They were not taught clearly that problems will still come, and that Satan will try to overcome them. We need to explain this plainly so they understand it, and then teach them how to use their spiritual weapons to overcome both Satan and the world.

FACING MISUNDERSTANDING

Jesus said, "If the world hate you, ye know that it hated me before it hated you" (John 15:18). He's telling us not to feel bad when people don't understand us, because long before they didn't understand us and hated us, they hated Him. This is a spiritual fact of the Christian life. Don't tell me you've lived as a Christian and have not been misunderstood. If you haven't been misunderstood, you haven't been living as a Christian. Being misunderstood is part of being a Christian.

Jesus said, "If ye were of the world, the world would love his own . . ." (John 15:19). Evil tends to get along with evil, and misery loves company. But evil has a hard time when righteousness shows up—darkness and light can't coexist. These opposites don't attract each other, they repel. Do you know why some people who work near you get upset? They can't cheat and get away with it when you're around—unless, of course, you're not living a holy life.

Jesus told His disciples,

> If ye were of the world, the world would love his own: but because ye are not of the world, but I have chosen you out of the world, therefore the world hateth you. Remember the word that I said unto you, The servant is not greater than his lord. If they have persecuted me, they will also persecute you; if they have kept my saying, they will keep yours also. But all these things will they do unto you for my name's sake, because they know not him that sent me (John 15:19-21).

They persecuted Jesus because they didn't know who sent Him, and if we belong to Christ and those we meet in our Christian walk don't know Him, many of them will treat us the same way. As Jesus indicated, there is not a different treatment for us than there was for Him.

When you're doing what pleases God, you'll find friends who also want to please God. God-pleasers attract one another and support one another. It's the "joy-quenchers" who try to "throw a wet blanket" over your enthusiasm. But Jesus told us that we shouldn't be upset over this. We shouldn't feel like we're being picked on. We shouldn't feel intimidated. He told us they did it to Him and the servant is not greater than his lord. The reason why they're doing these things is because He chose us out of the world. *That's Good News!*

THE GOD WHO IS THERE

> He that hateth me hateth my Father also. If I had not done among them the works which none other man did, they had not had sin: but now have they both seen and hated both me and my Father. But this cometh to pass, that the word might be fulfilled that is written in their law, They hated me without a cause (John 15:23-25).

You can be certain that if Jesus was hated without a cause, you will be also. But don't worry, the Comforter will be there to sustain you. "But when the Comforter is come, whom I will send unto you from the Father, even the Spirit of truth, which proceedeth from the Father, he shall testify of me" (John 15:26).

The Comforter is the Holy Spirit. He heals your infirmities, guides you into all truth, lives within you, and all His power and strength are available to you. He's here to give you comfort, peace, strength and guidance.

To all purposes, Jesus is telling us, "You may be struggling with a tough time right now, but when the

Comforter comes, He will permanently abide with you. His strength, His guidance, His comfort, and His direction will be within you and around you. He will give you the strength, the power and the ability to overcome every circumstance that life brings to you!"

That's why I believe praying in tongues is so powerful: "Likewise the Spirit also helpeth us in our infirmities: for we do not know what we pray for as we ought: but the Spirit itself maketh intercession for us with groanings that cannot be uttered" (Rom. 8:26). When you pray in tongues, your mind is unfruitful, but you pray with your spirit. By praying in the Spirit, we're praying the will of God. Out of your mouth you're praying the will of God in another tongue. In your head you may be thinking your own will. But through tongues, God bypasses your brain, thereby enabling you to pray out of your spirit.

DON'T BE OFFENDED

You have to face situations and people with truth and faith. Jesus hasn't taken you "out of the world," but He will always take you through the world with victory. Remember, the misery in others loves company. Discouraged people want you to be discouraged, too. Poor people want you to be poor with them. Such people don't rejoice with you when God gives you a new car. They're jealous when you get a better job or a new house. Don't be offended by their negativity.

The word offended is an incredible word. Years ago, when I was growing up, we used to use the word scandalized. You don't hear that word much anymore, but it's a biblical word. The word *offended* is the Greek word *skandaliz*. It means to be highly offended to the point of leaving and forsaking what you started doing.

Jesus taught it another way in Mark 4:15-17. He said that when the seed is sown, and persecutions and afflictions come against you because of the Word, you become easily offended. If you're going to get anywhere in God, you have to be tough, you have to be strong—you can't go around being offended all the time. The Apostle Paul said it this way, "Be strong in the Lord and in the power of His might" (Eph. 6:10). This is not optional—it's a command.

Many churches make some things of God optional. Some people say, "You don't really need the baptism of the Holy Spirit." If they mean in order to be saved, they're right. But you need the baptism of the Holy Spirit to live victoriously in your spiritual inheritance right now, and in the New Covenant rights of your salvation. The Scriptures command, "And be not drunk with wine, wherein is excess; but be filled with the Spirit" (Eph. 5:18). God knows that when we're filled with the Holy Spirit, we'll have the strength and power to face any adversity.

Even if someone deliberately tries to get to you, don't be offended, just pray in the Holy Ghost. Then tell yourself, "You can't put me down. You can't stop me. You can't hinder me from reaching my goal in God. My destiny is Canaan. There's no way you're going to stop me from proceeding in God, because I have the Comforter within me. I have the One who is called alongside to help. He'll help me and instruct me and guide me and empower me. He'll give me all I need to reach my goal in God."

Never forget that you have the Comforter within you. He'll make up for every lack in your life. Being intimidated is not easy for anyone. When people intimidate you, insult you, put you down, talk about you, do everything imaginable against you, it's not easy to take. Jesus rose above it. He set His face toward Jerusalem as a flint (Isa. 50:7). His powerful, over-coming Spirit now dwells within you!

Young pastors come to me and ask, "Can you give us the formula of success for starting a church?" There's no easy answer to that question. It takes a lot of prayer, preparation and perspiration. Those are the three P's of church growth. It takes WORK. It takes the determination that faith brings. When someone tells me I can't accomplish a goal that God has given me, I don't get offended, I get motivated! The church I pastor was built by God's people for $784,000.00. Construction companies had quoted us a cost of $2.2 million, but we saved $1.4 million because there was a group of people who said, "We can do it," and weren't offended by all the critics who said we couldn't do it.

There were times during the construction when I felt like Nehemiah. People would pass by and say, "Old Wacko is working out there in the cold and snow again." I remember one of our men shoveling snow all day so we could keep working.

A sub-contractor had told us, "We can't come back. There's too much snow."

We told him, "You be here tomorrow, there won't be one flake on the deck." And there wasn't!

After meeting such a construction challenge, it seems insignificant when someone complains, "He didn't shake my hand. I'm going to find a church where they love me." What are your eyes fixed upon? The Bible says we're to look unto Jesus. Too often we look at the circumstances or at each other. Jesus told us not to be discouraged, offended, scandalized or touchy.

Let's mature in our Christianity, stop being so easily offended, and together get on with God's work.

STANDING AND BELIEVING

This is where we run into trouble, and why some of your religious friends can't understand you. You speak the Word, preach the Word, live the Word, play tapes of the Word, confess the Word, read books about the Word, talk the Word and pray in tongues. Those Christians who don't, look at you and say, "What *is* the matter with you? Have you gone nuts?"

Can you imagine Bible-believing, tongue-talking, Holy Ghost-filled, King James-carrying, Charismaniacs telling you, "What's the matter with you? Have you gone crazy? You've been reading the Bible too much. That Bible is going to make you nuts." I've heard that over and over again. "You better unplug those tapes. You're getting too many Scriptures in you. Don't go overboard on your doctrine."

Certainly they are right to say you ought to be listening to things that edify and build you up, but their judgmental attitude is the problem. Religion is going to come against real Holy Ghost people. They're going to challenge your faith, your confession, your strong stand in believing God at all costs. "What's the matter? Are you crazy? Believing God to do that for you? Don't you know God chooses the ones He wants to heal?" Some people will talk you out of the blessing of God, if you let them. But Jesus said: "If ye abide in me, and my words abide in you, ye shall ask what ye will, and it shall be done unto you. Herein is my Father glorified . . ." (John 15:7-8).

In other words, God gets glory out of His people being blessed. I am not only talking about finances. A person with a bad marriage can get blessed by his or her marriage getting better. A person who doesn't have a job can be blessed by getting a job. A person who is depressed can be blessed by getting out of that depression. There are all kinds of blessings.

Faith is necessary in a real world. We do not live in a papier-mâché world. Jesus showed us how to deal with life. He said, "The Comforter, the Holy Ghost, will help you. He'll assist you. When you do not know what to do, He'll tell you what to do." The Holy Ghost will help you in situations where you have no understanding, where you can't figure things out in the natural. The Spirit of God will always help you if you allow your faith to hear what He is saying. Remember what Paul wrote:

> Likewise the Spirit also helpeth our infirmities [infirmities mean weaknesses, not sicknesses]: . . . for we know not what we should pray for as we ought: but the Spirit itself maketh intercession for us with groanings which cannot be uttered [words that can't be articulated in our language]. And he that searcheth the hearts knoweth what is the mind of the Spirit because he maketh intercession for the saints according to the will of God (Rom. 8:26-27).

71

Jesus wants us to know that since the day of Pentecost 2000 years ago, Christians have had the spiritual strength, ability and power to overcome every sorrow, woe, temptation, test, trial and circumstance that come their way because the Comforter He sent came to help us and strengthen us.

As I pray in tongues and thereby allow the Holy Spirit to pray the will of God through me, my head may be thinking all sorts of nutty things, but the Holy Ghost is praying the will of God. This is how I can encourage myself and cultivate my faith.

All things work together for good in your life. Not just some things. Not almost all things. Not a little bit. All things are always working together for your good because you love God and are called according to His purpose. Sometimes believing this is difficult, but faith apprehends this truth. God is always working His purpose out in your life for good.

There is nothing to be discouraged about when we choose to encourage ourselves in the Lord by His Holy Spirit.

When we learn to see things from His perspective and choose His way and will, everything looks different and is different.

God loves you and He will make you able to stand every test.

Always choose to walk in His way and His will by the power of the Holy Ghost.

6

Encourage Yourself in the Lord

GOD HAS A PLAN

Once God gives you His plan for your life, He never alters it. People will try to change it, the devil will try to talk you out of it, and you may become discouraged when life presents you with a lot of tough times, but God's plan will stay the same. The message of faith hasn't always told about the tough times we'll face. Our faith is for a purpose. As we exercise and increase our faith in the Word, God is equipping us to carry out His plan.

King David knew about tough times. When he was a young boy, David's family was visited by the prophet Samuel. The Lord had said to Samuel, "fill thine horn with oil, and go; I will send thee to Jesse the Bethlehemite: for I have provided me a King among his sons" (1 Sam. 16:1).

When Samuel got to Jesse's house, Jesse brought all his older sons to Samuel for consideration, but none of them was God's choice. Samuel asked Jesse if he had any more sons, so Jesse told him about his youngest, who was tending sheep:

> . . . And he said, There remaineth yet the youngest, and, behold, he keepeth the sheep. And Samuel said unto Jesse, Send and fetch him: for we will not sit down till he come hither. And he sent, and brought him in. Now he was ruddy and withal of a beautiful countenance, and goodly to look to. And the Lord said, Arise, anoint him: for this is he. Then Samuel took the horn of oil, and anointed him in the midst of his brethren: and the Spirit of the Lord came upon David from that day forward. So Samuel rose up, and went to Ramah (1 Sam. 16:11-13).

If that happened to us, we'd start looking for the prophecy to be fulfilled immediately. But it was about fifteen years before David became king. It takes sanctified tenacity and intestinal fortitude to hang in there when God gives you a promise and you don't see it manifested for over fifteen years.

David had tough times to go through before becoming king. Everywhere he went, King Saul was after him and even tried to kill him. He was jealous of David. David often had to hide in caves and run away from his pursuers.

First Samuel, chapter 29, tells about David and his soldiers fighting with the Philistine army. King Achish, had previously given David the southern part of their land, called Ziklag, where he was to live with his family. This must have been a relief to David, who had been on the run for a long time while being pursued by Saul. In

Ziklag, God blessed David; and while he and his men were there, they became warriors in Achish's army and fought for him.

But after a while, some of the Philistine lords complained to King Achish about David:

> Then Achish called David, and said unto him, Surely, as the LORD liveth, thou hast been upright, and thy going out and thy coming in with me in the host is good in my sight: for I have not found evil in thee since the day of thy coming unto me unto this day: nevertheless the lords favour thee not. Wherefore now return, and go in peace, that thou displease not the lords of the Philistines (1 Sam. 29:6-7).

Talk about injustice—what was fair about this? It must have been a tough time for David, just when he was beginning to feel secure, he was told to get out. Take a close look at David's life—it was filled with tough times. No matter how much God has anointed you, how much of the Word of God is in you, how wonderfully God has gifted you, you still have to face life's realities. And, sometimes, no matter how much you've done for people, they'll reject you.

Listen to what David said to Achish:

> . . . But what have I done? and what hast thou found in thy servant so long as I have been with thee unto this day, that I may not go fight against the enemies of my lord the king? And Achish answered and said to David, I know that thou art good in my sight, as an angel of God . . . (1 Sam. 29:8-9).

How's that for a recommendation? The king saw

David as an angel of God. How would you like to have that as your testimony to the world, to have others say that you're an angel of God to them? That is what God has called the Church to be—a light in a dark world; salt in a tasteless society; an honorable example to a dishonorable society.

One of the factors about David that must have impressed the king most of all was that since David had been with him, the king's army had not experienced defeat. Nonetheless, the king still commanded David to go.

> . . . notwithstanding the princes of the Philistines have said, He shall not go up with us to the battle. Wherefore now rise up early in the morning with thy master's servants that are come with thee: and as soon as ye be up early in the morning, and have light, depart. So David and his men rose up early to depart in the morning, to return into the land of the Philistines. And the Philistines went up to Jezreel (1 Sam. 29:9-11).

What a journey that must have been. David was going home after another rejection, another disappointment, another despondency, another discouragement. One important difference between someone who makes it in God and someone who does not make it is how much the individual permits past failures to influence them

David could have said, "I've had enough dis-appointment. Life is throwing me all kinds of foul balls and lemons. I can't take it anymore. How can I face another discouragement? All I've done is help others, and still people treat me unfairly and talk badly about me. What's the point of trying? I can't even live here any longer." That was one alternative he could have taken. Instead, he chose to face the tough time with faith in his good God. However, David's tough times had just started.

> And it came to pass, when David and his men were come to Ziklag on the third day, that the Amalekites had invaded the south, and Ziklag, and smitten Ziklag, and burned it with fire; And had taken the women captives, that were therein: they slew not any, either great or small, but carried them away, and went on their way (1 Sam. 30:1-2).

When David and his men returned home, they received worse news than before. Forget about the rejection they had experienced. Now they learned that their city had been burned and their families had been taken captive. They beheld the ruins of Ziklag. Like Job, they had lost everything. Some of us will lose some things, others will lose many things—but few people lose everything!

Look carefully at what happened when David walked back into the city:

> So David and his men came to the city, and, behold, it was burned with fire; and their wives, and their sons, and their daughters, were taken captives. Then David and the people that were with him lifted up their voice and wept, until they had no more power to weep (1 Sam. 30:3-4).

Like most of us probably would have done in the face of such circumstance, David said, "I can't take it anymore. Oh, God!" *AND HE WEPT UNTIL THERE WAS NO MORE POWER OR STRENGTH TO WEEP!*

ENCOURAGING YOUR SOUL

I have a feeling that if some 20th century faith heroes had been there they would have said, "Would you look at him! No faith. Listen to him—a man anointed of God and crying like a baby."

David, like Jesus and Jeremiah and so many others, wept. Like us, they were people with emotions. We're not only spirit, we are also SOUL and body. My soul is the seat of my emotions. When you pinch my skin, I get bruised. When my soul is wounded, I hurt. It hurts to feel rejection and it hurts to see that everything you have lived for has been wiped away. We cannot deny the reality of pain at such a time.

Furthermore, David's tough times weren't over yet—things got worse:

> And David was greatly distressed; for the people spake of stoning him, because the soul of all the people was grieved, every man for his sons and for his daughters . . . (1 Sam. 30:6).

When things go bad, people always look for someone to blame—a Jonah to throw overboard, a Christ to crucify. David had been rejected by King Achish. He then returned home to discover that his wives and children were gone and his house burned down. Now, to top it off, his home-town friends wanted to kill him. Did this anointed man of God have something to be distressed about?

Most of us would have "gotten off" the train by this time. We would probably have said, "Enough is enough is enough! All I ever get for serving God is trouble." I've often heard Christians say something like, "All I ever get for serving God is situations I don't know what to do with. I trust God and look what happens to me."

David was distressed beyond measure, but he pulled himself out of it by doing what we should all do in tough times: *". . . David encouraged himself in the LORD his God"* (1 Sam. 30:6). Hallelujah!

There are two alternatives when you get distressed because of tough times. You get bitter, or you get better. Too often, we want our strength and our help to come from other Christians, but no human being can give us the spiritual hope and strength that we need—as David well knew and proclaimed:

> Blessed be the LORD: for he hath shewed me his marvelous kindness in a strong city. For I said in my haste, I am cut off from before thine eyes: nevertheless thou heardest the voice of my supplications when I cried unto thee. O love the LORD, all ye his saints: for the LORD preserveth the faithful, and plentifully rewardeth the proud doer. Be of good courage, and he shall strengthen your heart, all ye that hope in the LORD (Ps. 31:21-24).

David once wrote about himself, "My tears have been my meat day and night . . ." (Ps. 42:3). In other words, "I couldn't even eat because of the sorrow I felt on the inside." He probably felt that way right about now in his life. And maybe you do, too. One thing is certain, you won't go through this life unscathed. Perhaps you suffered rejection on your job. You were in line for a promotion you deserved and didn't get it. Or you've been the victim of racism or violence. Maybe you've been discriminated against. Or someone misunderstood you, talked about you, slandered you. Or perhaps you were abused or rejected as a child. Whatever tough times you've had in your life, you're probably familiar with what David meant when he said that tears had been his meat day and night. If you are, remember what David's response was to the tough time he was going through at the moment:

> And David was greatly distressed; for the people spake of stoning him, because the soul of all the people was grieved, every man for his sons and for his daughters: *BUT DAVID ENCOURAGED HIMSELF IN THE LORD HIS GOD* (1 Sam. 30:6, emphasis mine).

David encouraged himself in the Lord his God. This is what God's people *must* do in tough times. The Psalms show us how David encouraged himself in the Lord:

> Behold, the eye of the LORD is upon them that fear him, upon them that hope in his mercy; to deliver their soul from death, and to keep them alive in famine. Our soul waiteth for the LORD: he is our help and our shield. For our heart shall rejoice in him, because we have trusted in his holy name. Let thy mercy, O LORD, be upon us, according as we hope in thee (Ps. 33:18-22).

David may have remembered all that God had done for him, and how Samuel came to his father's house and anointed him with oil—he may have remembered feeling the power of that anointing upon him time and again. Perhaps that's why he wrote at another time,

80

> Why art thou cast down, O my soul? and why art thou disquieted in me? hope thou in God: for I shall yet praise him for the help of his countenance. O my God, my soul is cast down within me: therefore will I remember thee from the land of Jordan, and of the Hermonites, from the hill Mizar (Ps. 42:5-6).

A child of God is like a sheep that needs to constantly be eating and drinking. There's no time for a sheep to be cast down. If you stop eating and drinking—eating the Word, drinking the Word, feeding on the Word, being refreshed—you get cast down and lose your hope in God.

David was saying, in effect, "I'm going to go back and rehearse all the good things you have done for me, Lord." The same practical truth was expressed by a gospel song: "When I remember what He has done for me, I can never turn back again."

The problem with many of us is that we don't remember the goodness of God in our lives. We forget where God has brought us from and where He is taking us. So, when a difficult situation arises, we are ill-equipped to deal with it.

REMEMBERING GOD'S GOODNESS

We need to be more like David and *encourage ourselves in the Lord.* I'm not going to encourage myself in the Lord if I am going to let another Christian talk me out of God's blessings. How am I going to encourage myself in the Lord if I listen to a someone who says, "Well, you know, it happens that way to all of us"?

I need someone who says to me, "Brother, I'm in

there with you. Bless God, the Lord is your hope. He is your strength. He is your joy and peace." Positive affirmations of faith like that bring hope to a troubled heart and healing to a sick body.

I remember several years ago when we were praying for some people with sickle cell anemia. A lady said to me one day, "Well, you know, this disease runs in our culture."

I told her, "I don't receive that in the name of Jesus!" She got angry with me, but her daughter got healed. God is greater than cultural, societal, racial, national tendencies. He's brought us into a new culture: the Kingdom of God!

You don't want to be around people who are going to talk you out of the blessings of God. Get away from people who have a negative confession. Get by yourself if you have to. David did. He didn't have anyone to help him, so he encouraged HIMSELF in the Lord. There are going to be times when you don't have anyone around you. At those times, you'd better know God. You'd better know who He is. You'd better remember what He has done for you and believe what He can do. You'd better say to Him, "God, I'm trusting you. I can't look to the left or to the right. I don't have anyone to help me. I'm trusting you!"

David pulled his soul up short and confronted it: "Why art thou down cast, O my soul? And why art thou disquieted in me?"

Did you ever feel as if somebody inside was talking to you? Your emotions and your feelings sometimes do talk to you. David's soul was saying, "You're not going to make it. Nothing good is going to happen to you. How are you going to get your family back? Everyone is against you and wants to kill you"

His soul was disquieted within him. Have you ever laid down in bed at night and said, "God, thank you for this day." Then, because your soul was not quieted or convinced—you had not recognized and dealt with its restlessness before you retired—five minutes later you were in a turmoil. You were under the covers, on top of the covers, fluffed the pillow, pounded the pillow, got up, got a drink, went to the bathroom, went back to bed, tossed and turned, turned and tossed. Your soul was disquieted and it wasn't going to let the rest of you be quiet and sleep, either. Misery loves company.

All this may have happened because your rent is due, your job situation isn't what you'd like it to be, someone hurt your feelings, there are problems between you and your wife—in other words, there is something wrong in your life and it's worrying you. You are unsettled! Get up, grab your Bible and begin to encourage yourself in the Lord like David did. You can take dominion over your soul. If the devil has been beating on you, he'll quit and hope you leave him alone when he sees that you're going to pray and read the Word.

TRUST IN GOD

I want to be around people who encourage me. I don't want to be around grumpy people who bring gloom to others. I don't want to be around people who bad-mouth the things of God. "Oh, you mean you really believe in this faith stuff?"

I always want my answer to be, "Yes, and I'm not

listening to your junk. I'll stand for the Word that builds up my faith."

My strong stand has caused hundreds of people to leave the doors of the church I pastor. I love those folks and I thank God they had a time when we could minister to them, but I'm not changing to suit them. I know where I came from, I know what God brought me out of, I know what this message of faith has done in my life and I'm not going back to the past.

"Well, it hasn't worked for me," someone will say. I respond, "that's because you haven't acted on your faith, you aren't living it, and you haven't been walking it out.

David encouraged himself in the Lord. He said, "I refuse to have this situation eat me up." So he took command of his soul, looked to God for mercy, praised His word, and put his trust in Him.

> Be merciful unto me, O God: for man would swallow me up; he fighting daily oppresseth me. Mine enemies would daily swallow me up: for they be many that fight against me, O thou most High. What time I am afraid, I will trust in thee. In God I will praise his word, in God I have put my trust; I will not fear what flesh can do unto me (Ps. 56:1-4).

You may say, "Well, I'm not David. I don't have the same kind of life he did." True enough. Your life is probably far less dangerous and discouraging. But your life is not one bit less valuable and precious to God! David is no better than you in the kingdom. God loves each of us equally. You can say, "Lord God, you called me, saved me, and brought me out. You filled me with the Holy Ghost. You brought me into the kingdom. I am your son. I am your daughter. Lord, I am looking to you. I trust you. I cannot trust man. I cannot lean on man. I cannot look to man. You are my God!" Learn to trust in God and encourage yourself in the Lord like David did.

ENCOURAGING YOURSELF IN THE LORD

> And David said to Abiathar the priest, Ahimelech's son, I pray thee, bring me hither the ephod. And Abiathar brought thither the ephod to David. [The linen ephod was a sign of holiness.] And David enquired at the LORD, saying, Shall I pursue after this troop? shall I overtake them? . . . (1 Sam. 30:7-8).

This is how you talk when you're encouraging yourself in the Lord. You don't ask why something has happened to you, you ask: *"WHAT DO YOU WANT ME TO DO NOW, GOD? WHAT SHALL I PURSUE?"* You don't pray these kind of prayers, "Oh God, somehow, someway, with just a little of Your mercy and grace . . . please something . . . I am so unworthy, but I love you."

David didn't pray that way. He said, "By my authority, let me have the ephod. I'm going before the Father." Then David got before the Father and said, "Shall I pursue after this troop? Shall I overtake them?" Notice that David wasn't saying "what shall we do," he was saying "what shall I do." He wanted to know what he should do, not what everyone else should do. ". . . And he [God] answered him, Pursue: for thou shalt surely overtake them and without fail recover all" (1 Sam. 30:8).

When we call upon the Lord, He answers us. He told Jeremiah to record for all ages that He wanted His people to call out to Him: "Call unto me, and I will answer thee, and shew thee great and mighty things, which thou knowest not" (Jer. 33:3). The reason God is not answering some of us is that we're not calling on Him.

"Oh, but I call on God," someone remarks, "but I still don't get an answer." I'm talking about calling on Him in faith. I'm not talking about some weak kind of prayer. I'm talking about a prayer that says, "I know you'll be with me, God, so shall I pursue this troop? Shall I overtake them?"

God promised David that if he'd do his part and pursue, God would enable him to recover all. Too many of us have settled for a part instead of all. You can recover all that you have lost. The key is to pursue.

Pursue Your Goals

You and I don't have a single circumstance in our life that God can't resolve. The problem is that we fail to go to Him. We try every other approach. We go to recovery groups, read self-help books, go to therapy and try every avenue except the one that really works—pursuing our goals by faith with God at our side.

Someone might comment, "Well, praise the Lord. I'm just happy serving the Lord. Isn't it wonderful to have the peace of God?" This is a good affirmation. But what is its power if you can't pay your bills and you're unhealthy? What is its power if your stomach aches, your head aches and everything else aches, too? What is its power if you spend more money on doctors than you give in the offering? We can pursue our goals by faith, and this will encourage us in the Lord

After God told David to "pursue," David fasted and prayed for five weeks to make sure he'd heard the voice of God. His prayer not only strengthened and encouraged him, but his prayer got his men's act together as well. They went from wanting to stone him to going out to fight for him.

God is our source. When we don't know how to handle something in the natural and we don't have answers in our own human wisdom, there is a Power we can plug into. That divine current will flow, and it will change the hearts of people and situations and things that we don't know what to do about!

Always remember: what God did for David, He will do for us:

> And David recovered all that the Amalekites had carried away: and David rescued his two wives (1 Sam. 30:18).

God will restore families. He'll bring husbands and wives home. He'll bring children back. He'll restore the finances that have been stolen by the enemy. His Word to His people today is, "Arise! Pursue! Seek me! Trust me! I will surely do what I said I would do. I will not fail you!"

The devil is a defeated foe!

The battle has been won!

Jesus is still on the throne!

Encourage yourself in the Lord your God and then pursue!

7

Reaching Your Destiny

Every human being is special and important to God—valuable and precious in His sight—both the believer and the unbeliever. The Scripture says, "For God so loved the world . . ." (John 3:16).

COMMIT YOUR WAY TO GOD

David wrote that if you commit your way to the Lord, and trust in Him, He will bring it to pass (Ps. 37:5). Several years ago, I listened to a tape by Dr. Ken Stewart entitled "Daydreaming With the Holy Ghost." From it, I learned that a lot of us don't know how to dream. We have no vision for what God intends our lives to become. We look at life like Doris Day did in the song *"Que Sera Sera*—whatever will be, will be." Many Christians approach life from the perspective, "If I make it, fine. If I don't, fine. We're all going to heaven some day anyway."

That passive philosophy sounds right, but it's wrong. Your active part in God's plan is so important that if you miss knowing and cooperating with God in bringing forth what He has for you, you could negatively affect not only your life, but the lives of a whole lot of other people.

The Bible says that God will bless your way; that is, His way for you. God's not going to bless your way if it has nothing to do with Him. Your way must be committed to God, or to what God has placed in your heart.

It's sad to see someone who comes to the end of his or her life without fulfilling the vision or dream God imparted to them. They've allowed certain things to occupy their lives, to hinder and stop them from reaching their place in God. If you want to know God's plan for you, start with the sacred Book that imparts His will and His wisdom. Pray His Word and let His promises soak into your spirit.

Do you know why people don't think about God correctly? It's because they don't read the Word. They've only heard what other people *think* about the Word. They don't realize that only the Scriptures can give us a proper understanding of God. If you've received your concept of God from Aunt Mable and Uncle Joe and Preacher Jones, and you haven't received your concept of God from His Word, you probably have a distorted understanding of God.

If your concept of God is faulty, you'll never understand His love for you, or His plan or purpose for your life. You'll always have a distorted view based upon what other people think God is doing for you.

Your friends and your relatives, even your spiritual leaders, can't tell you what God's plan for your life is—only God can do that. God prepares the plan and He reveals it to you. All of us come into this life with "sealed orders" from the Creator. To open His orders, we need the tools of His Word, prayer, worship and fellowship.

If God isn't talking to you, that's because you haven't been talking to Him and then listening for the answer. You haven't tuned into His frequency. You talk to everybody else to try to find the will of God for you. You ask others, "What do you think the will of God is for my life?" Instead of going to others, go directly to the Lord.

What God Thinks About You

Here is what God thinks about you:

> For I know the plans I have for you, declares the Lord. Plans to prosper you and not to harm you, plans to give you a hope and a future (Jer. 29:11 NIV).

That's what God thinks about us. He's talking to Israel here about their restoration from captivity, but the principle applies to us as well. Israel had been in Babylonian captivity for seventy years, and God told them He was going to bring them out of captivity and into a place where they were going to be prosperous and good would come to them. God's plans for us are the same—for good and not for evil.

GOD'S NOT YOUR PROBLEM

Have you ever heard someone say, "God took my baby," or, "God took my father."? Perhaps an accident victim has testified, "God put me in a wreck," or someone says, "God gave me cancer," or "I have this arthritis because God is punishing me." These are the kinds of statements some people have made. God does not kill people or give people cancer or arthritis. He wants to prosper you and give you a future and a hope.

I'm a channel-flipper when I'm watching TV. I get twelve Christian networks on my satellite dish and flip between all of them. One evening I saw a preacher on a program who was showing the Midwest floods of 1993. He was describing the scene that showed ugly pictures of people moving their things out of their houses, and houses floating away. Then he said, "This is God judging America!" That kind of talk makes me angry.

Do you remember when Jesus was caught in the storm? The Bible says He rebuked the wind and the waves. The Greek word used there for "rebuke" is the same word Jesus used to rebuke the devil when He first preached in His Galilean ministry. If the storm had come from His heavenly Father, then Jesus would have been accused of rebuking His own Father. Storms are not acts of God, and neither is sickness or poverty or defeat. What insurance companies call "acts of God" are actually "acts of the devil." God is not the author of disaster.

Regrettably, many unbelievers think God causes evil. Even some Christians have that concept of God. In fact, the world would not have its distorted view of God if it hadn't learned it from the Church. Is it any wonder that in a time of tragedy, both saints and sinners often ask, "Why did God do this to me?" But even though they think wrongly of God, God knows His own thoughts toward us, and they are for good and not evil.

You'll hear some Christians say, "Oh, but when I went to the hospital as a patient, God spoke to me." I'm sure He did, but God wanted to speak to that person before they got sick, but because they didn't want to listen, they ended up in the hospital. When you're on your back and have no one else to talk to, you'll sometimes hear God's voice. But don't say that God put you there. To imply that is to say that God is ugly, mean, and cruel because He did that to you.

God thinks peace and good about you, not evil. Is sickness evil? Is poverty evil? Are floods evil? Those are questions that need no answers for those who truly know the God who is love.

PEOPLE OF DESTINY

God has a destiny for your life. How can you understand what God wants you to do if you don't know Him? As I said before, the Scriptures initiate our concept of God. God says, "My thoughts for you are good." God is not your enemy, He's your best Friend.

Please understand that I don't know everything there is to know about God. Some things can't be explained.

> The secret things belong unto the LORD our God: but those things which are revealed belong unto us and to our children for ever, that we may do all the words of this law (Deut. 29:29).

93

God, in effect, says that we have no business looking into some things. What He reveals to us belongs to us forever, but the secret things belong to Him. Only He knows which are which and He will reveal to you that which you need to know when you need to know it. Yet we keep on questioning Him, sometimes in an almost accusatory manner: "Why did that happen?" or "Why did that person die so young?"

At such times we should simply continue to believe God and love Him. The rest is really none of our business. God has a plan for my life, and He is continually working His purposes out. My responsibility is to take care of me according to His plan for me—and most of us have a hard enough time doing that.

> Many, O LORD my God, are thy wonderful works which thou hast done, and thy thoughts which are to us-ward: they cannot be reckoned up in order unto thee: if I would declare and speak of them, they are more than can be numbered (Ps. 40:5).

FOLLOWING GOD'S PLAN

Many of God's people have missed the plan and purpose of God for their lives because they never took the time to find out what God has in store for them. Many have missed the best things God had for them because they were so occupied with the minutia of life: worried about how they feel, how much money they have, what other people might think about them, etc. "The fear of man bringeth a snare: but whoso putteth his trust in the Lord shall be safe" (Prov. 29:25).

Many good people of God have been caught in traps

94

of their own making, preventing them from fulfilling God's plan for their lives. To know what God's purpose is for your life, you have to go back to the original plan recorded in the first book in the Bible:

> . . . Let us make man in our image, after our likeness: and let them have dominion over the fish of the sea, and over the fowl of the air, and over the cattle, and over all the earth, and over every creeping thing that creepeth upon the earth. So God created man in his own image, in the image of God created he him; male and female created he them. And God blessed them, and God said unto them, *Be fruitful, and multiply, and replenish the earth, and subdue it: and have dominion over the fish of the sea, and over the fowl of the air, and over every living thing that moveth upon the earth* (Gen. 1:26-28, italics mine).

God blessed first. Then He told mankind to be fruitful and multiply, replenish the earth, and subdue it. He wanted us to take dominion over His creation. That's what He told us to do.

If we're to take dominion over creation, why do some Christians say, "I'm just a poor, old, weak worm of the dust who was saved by grace. I'm on my way to heaven, washed in the blood. Praise God, I don't have much here, but when I get to heaven . . . ." Their problem is that it's easier to believe a poverty message than a prosperity message because so many people are poor. (Sometimes we explain things theologically by situations.) But God's thoughts for you are for good, not evil, to give you an end with expectation, a future, a hope. God wants to bless you!

This doesn't mean we're all supposed to be millionaires. To some people, rich means having a lot of money. To others, rich means having enough money and good health. To still others, rich is a good family, a healthy marriage and having children who serve God—these people are truly rich.

Solomon may have been the richest man who will ever live, but he was miserable. Money doesn't buy you happiness. God's plan isn't for us to be super-rich, but to dominate, rule, control, subdue and conquer His creation. Yet, in the face of such truth, many Christians just keep tiptoeing through life saying, "I hope God has something for me to do . . . I hope someday there will be a future out there for me, somewhere." If you're that kind of Christian, remember: God only blesses us in proportion to our faith.

GOD HAS NEVER ALTERED HIS ORIGINAL PLAN

Although God has never altered His original plan, someone did alter it: man. The authority God gave to man, Adam willingly gave to the devil. Satan didn't steal it from man as many have said, man gave it to him.

Many of us are spiritually doing the same thing today. We're surrendering the authority, the dominion, the power, the things God has given us. We're giving these things over to the devil and to the religious crowd because we're afraid to take a stand for what we believe God's will is for our lives.

When we arrive finally at the place of faith where we know our position and our inheritance in God, the same place God said Adam had, we don't have to worry about other things in our lives. You won't have to worry about negative situations or circumstances, how anyone treats you, what anyone thinks about you or what man does to you. You'll be able to refer back to God's plan in complete trust, because you'll know God's Word.

You need to start thinking and talking like this: "I am the head and not the tail. I am above and not beneath. I am blessed going in and going out. Everything I touch is blessed." Will everyone like you for saying that? Certainly not, but that won't matter to you.

David said that the Lord had done so many wonderful works for him that he couldn't even count them. I wonder how many times we've talked ourselves out of "wonderful works" of God by saying things like: "I'll never get that job." "I'm sure they are not giving any raises. I won't get this raise." "I can't afford that house." "I can't afford that car."

> If ye then be risen with Christ, seek those things which are above, where Christ sitteth on the right hand of God (Col. 3:1).

That's where our focus should be—on the eternal truths of God's Word. The Bible reveals God's plan to us.

A RENEWED IMAGE

> . . . put on the new man, which is renewed in knowledge after the image of him that created him (Col. 3:10).

I'm risen with Christ and have a new image—the image of Him who created me in His image. I've put on the new man.

97

The "old man" thought differently. The "old man" thought, "God is tough. God is mean. God will hit me on the head. He'll cause me to get in automobile accidents or have cancer if He wants to." But the new man is risen with Christ, seeks the things that are above, and his mind has been renewed to the image of Him who created him. What a contrast Paul paints for us in these verses in his epistle to the Colossians.

We used to sing an "old man" chorus:

> Just another touch, Lord, from you to help in hard trials I go through. Though dark may be the night, He sheds a ray of light. Just another touch, Lord, from you.

That song represents the concept many Christians have of themselves—just weary pilgrims on their way home, with their feet dragging, but still holding on. A Christian with that kind of perspective will say, "No matter how hard and trying my life is, He's going to bring me through. Oh, hallelujah." Bring them through to what?

In testimony services, people often get up and say something like, "The devil's been all over my back this week. My dryer broke, my car wouldn't start, and my kid left home. But, praise God, I'm saved."

How do you get a sinner saved who hears a testimony like that? How do you get a sinner to appreciate that Jesus truly is Lord over everything? Why doesn't the pastor straighten out their theology before Christians like these scare all the unsaved away? The fact is that many preachers are not able to preach the Word of God in truth and power because they're not living a life of victory themselves. You can't tell someone to go to a place (or a level) you've never gone yourself.

We need to be testifying about the God who loved us enough to make us in His own image. This is the God who is ready to put power into us through our faith so that we can dominate the earth. Why would anyone want to know a God that's presented as being mean, ugly and rotten—one who gives people sickness and takes their children away? No one would want to know a God like that.

PROBLEM-SOLVERS AND PROBLEM-MAKERS

> Christ hath redeemed us from the curse of the law
> ... Gentiles through Jesus Christ; that we might receive
> the promise of the Spirit through faith (Gal. 3:13-14).

We are redeemed! We have been bought back! Satan's curse no longer has power over us! The blessings of Abraham are ours!

I'm so tired of hearing Christians say, "Aren't things terrible? Aren't things awful? Oh, the drug addiction is so bad. Oh, I tell you. Everything in the world today is just getting so bad."

I like to fellowship with people who have solutions, not just problem updates. If you are a problem-solver, you're my friend. If you're a problem-maker, you're someone I'm going to stay away from. We ought to always surround ourselves with problem-solvers, people who have solutions, except in those specific cases where we are concentrating on comforting and uplifting another person. When you're doing that, remember to be prayed up and filled to the brim with God's truth. That way you won't have any little dark nooks and crannies that can catch gloom and discouragement. You'll give life and light without being diminished in any way by darkness and discouragement.

HEIRS ACCORDING TO GOD'S PROMISE

> And if ye be Christ's, then are ye Abraham's seed, and heirs *according to the promise* (Gal. 3:29, italics mine).

That promise goes back to Genesis 12. Genesis is the "Book of Beginnings." Everything God started is right there. He told Abraham that He was going to bless him so much that all the nations of the earth would be blessed through him. Thousands of years later, God told believers that they are now Abraham's seed, and that if they are Christ's, then they are Abraham's seed and heirs according to Genesis 12. That's God's promise to you and me.

God, in effect, is saying, "I didn't change my plan. You changed my plan. You've told others that I'm their enemy. You've told them I've been mad at them. You're the one who told them the flood came because I didn't like them and was judging them."

Don't tell anyone that God causes cancer, AIDS, floods, hurricanes, violence or any other tragedy. The Scripture says that the thief comes to steal, kill and destroy. The calamities of life are stealing and destroying. The thief is Satan, not God.

The devil is your enemy. He's the one who steals, kills and destroys marriages. He robs children away from us. He puts our kids on drugs. These things don't come from God. People cry out, "Then, why didn't God stop it?"

The answer to this heart-felt question is complex. The Bible says that Satan is the ruler of this world and that the only power he has is the power we allow him to have. Because the Christian Church has not been taught to take dominion, to take authority, to take power, we have drug addicts pushing the Church to the suburbs, pushing good people out of neighborhoods.

We fail to realize that the same devil that walks the city streets lurks in the country hills. Most of us are victims of a religious system that has lied about God! The only way this is going to change will be if we change our attitudes.

GETTING A NEW ATTITUDE

We change by believing the promises of the Word of God. We change by not letting anyone but God himself tell us (through His revealed Word) what our position and place in the world is today. "And if ye be Christ's, then are ye Abraham's seed . . . ." If I'm a part of Abraham's family, I can share in the blessings of Isaac and Jacob. I, too, can sow in famine and in the same year, reap a hundredfold return!

Yes, we're living in tough times, but as tough people we can take hold of the hand of our good God. He loves you and wants only good for you.

> Fret not thyself because of evildoers, neither be thou envious against the workers of iniquity. For they shall soon be cut down like the grass, and wither as the green herb. Trust in the LORD, and do good; so

shalt thou dwell in the land, and verily thou shalt be
fed (Ps. 37:1-3).

If the Spirit of God could just lift the level of our
expectations, we would see the plan of God for our lives.
We need to set our goals high; dream our dreams, see
our visions. Let's lift the level of our expectations,
having no doubts about God fulfilling His plan for our
lives.

Remember all of God's good promises to you.

They are not my promises, not Kenneth Copeland's,
not Kenneth Hagin's—they are God's direct promises
to you.

You cannot walk in faith when you doubt.

In the same way that doubt comes, it goes, but ". . .
faith cometh by hearing, and hearing by the Word of
God" (Rom. 10:17).

8

God Gives Good Gifts

GOD ISN'T YOUR PROBLEM—HE'S YOUR ANSWER

It's time for the Church to set the record straight about who God really is. He's a good God, and we need to announce this fact. God loves you! God's not your problem, He's your answer.

> Let no man say when he is tempted, I am tempted of God: for God cannot be tempted with evil, neither tempteth he any man (James 1:13).

God's not involved with anything evil. He's not promoting it or using it. God is incapable of doing evil in any way. He's not our tempter—Satan is.

> But every man is tempted [We know who the tempter is—Satan, not God], when he is drawn away of his own lust, and enticed (James 1:14).

In this verse, the blame isn't even put on the tempter. It's put on the Christian. In other words, I have the power to close or open the door to temptation. This is a simple fact, and yet many people overlook it.

THE BOTTOM LINE

If I'm having a problem with temptation in any form (it could be in any area of life—sexual, financial, relational, etc.), it is my own lust (strong desire) that draws me toward it. The word "lust" means an inordinate (exceeding reasonable limits, immoderate) amount of affection toward something.

James continues, "Do not err, my beloved brethren" (James 1:16). To err is to get into errors, mistakes, misjudgments, miscalculations and such. Notice that James isn't talking to those outside the Body of Christ. He's talking to believers. By so doing, James implies that error exists among Bible-believing Christians regarding the subject he's about to present.

One of the errors some Christians fall into was addressed by James in verse 1:13. That error involves blaming God when you're going through tough times. James wrote this epistle to believers who were under severe persecution. They were being tested for their faith.

Most of us are never truly tested for our faith. The areas in which we usually get tested concern whether we believe one doctrine or another. Usually no one challenges us for our faith. It's probably a good thing, too, because many of us don't want to defend what we believe when we're challenged. Usually people get challenged only when they challenge others, sometimes directly, and sometimes indirectly by the standards with which they live their lives. Do our lives present messages that challenge those who are in the world, especially about God who is the Giver of all good things?

> Every good gift and every perfect gift is from above, and cometh down from the Father of lights, with whom is no variableness, neither shadow of turning (James 1:17).

There are few Scripture verses that are clearer than this one in giving us a vivid picture of the character of God. This verse shows us why God cannot tempt us with evil: He is the Giver of good and perfect gifts only, and He never changes.

This passage teaches us many things about ourselves and about God:

Don't blame God when you're tempted.

Realize that failure happens when you're drawn away and are tempted by the tempter. To be drawn away, you have to agree with the one who's doing the drawing. If God doesn't tempt, then someone else does. We know from the Scriptures that Satan is the tempter.

God is a good God, and every good and perfect gift comes from the Father of lights, in whom there is no variableness. He never changes. What He starts out to do He always accomplishes. There is no shadow of turning with our loving heavenly Father. He does not turn His plan and purpose around. Everything God said originally He is still doing because He is incapable of changing His character. Even when man is evil, God remains good.

The devil is a liar, a deceiver, an accuser. The Bible clearly tells us that, "The thief cometh not, but for to steal, and to kill, and to destroy . . ." (John 10:10). There is nothing in the devil or in his schemes that is good. Killing, stealing and destroying are his constant goals.

Don't blame God for your tough times, He's not your problem, He's your answer—and your solution. You won't get anywhere in God until you realize that if you're sick, He didn't cause it. He's the One who wants to heal you. If you're poor, God didn't cause your poverty. He's the One who wants to bless you financially. If you're depressed, God didn't cause it. He wants to lift it from you and give you abundant life. Every good gift comes from above. Every evil gift comes from the devil. That's why God sent His Son—to take care of the devil and all his evil. The work of our Lord and Savior is to destroy, reduce to zero and paralyze the work of the devil. "For this purpose the Son of God was manifested, that he might destroy the works of the devil" (1 John 3:8).

DON'T JUDGE OTHERS

> Therefore thou art inexcusable, O man, whosoever thou art that judgest: for wherein thou judgest another, thou condemnest thyself; for thou that judgest doest the same things (Rom. 2:1).

We need to be careful that we don't judge others. When you point your finger at someone, always remember that you have three fingers pointing back at you. Once I heard a man add a line to this expression: "They all have nails in them, too!" Only God can truly judge because only He knows the ultimate truth of anything.

There are always three sides to every story: your side, my side, and the right side. The right side, of course, is God's side. God is pure and He judges everyone according to truth. He establishes the boundaries within which He acts according to who He is. He is incapable of acting in any way that goes outside the boundaries of His character. He judges everything by truth. He cannot lie, and He cannot do evil.

It is so important to understand that He does not judge you according to what you do. He judges you by your inner character—who you really are. Thank God for that, because some people are right in their hearts, but they are really messed up in their heads.

Please don't misunderstand me. God has reserved judgment and punishment for those who blaspheme Him, those who willfully step out of line, but the majority of people who miss God don't miss Him because they want to or because they deliberately choose to do so. They just don't know how to get to Him because they've never been taught. They've listened to so many messages of condemnation and judgment that they're not even sure if God wants them near Him.

God's love for us is not based upon the way we act. Making a mistake doesn't cause God to stop loving the people He created. What kind of a God and heavenly Father would He be if every time we did something wrong He said, "Well, you've made a mistake; you've sinned, so I'm not going to love you anymore." That's the way we sometimes act, but God never responds to His people that way. Our wonderful Father just keeps on loving us. It's as if He says, "They're my children. I love them. I don't like what they doing, but I am not going to stop loving them." As parents, don't we do this with out kids, too? Do you think God is going to fall out of love with us because we sinned this week? The Holy Ghost in you will make you feel miserable when you sin, and your close fellowship with God gets a little distance put into it. But God still loves you, just as you still love your spouse even when you've had a quarrel over something.

You can't lose your relationship with God. My earthly father and mother could have given me up for adoption when I was born, but that wouldn't have changed the fact that they were my parents. I would have been out of fellowship with them, to be sure, but the blood relationship would have remained.

Jesus said, ". . . No man is able to pluck them out of my father's hand" (John 10:29). The Scriptures indicate that God is fastened to the backslider. Even Israel, which forsook God and betrayed Him and helped to put Jesus on the Cross, is being restored to fellowship with the Father. God loves all those who are in His family.

So many people think when something goes wrong, "I missed it. I lost it. I am not saved anymore." This is simply not true. See what the Scripture says:

> There is therefore now no condemnation to them which are in Christ Jesus, who walk not after the flesh, but after the Spirit (Rom. 8:1-2).

We are blessed that our Father is not a man that He should lie. He is not like a human being. You might have met someone in your life who doesn't love you anymore after you made a mistake, but you're not talking about human responses when you're talking about Father God.

Most human relationships are based on trust and feelings that have to do with "what I do for you" and "what you do for me." Our relationship with God, however, is not based on what we do for Him; it's not by works that we have done, but it's by His grace that we're saved. God did not save us because of who we are or what we did, He saved us because *HE LOVES US!* We should constantly praise Him that He judges us according to *His* character, and not the way we judge each other, or we would all be condemned.

> And thinkest thou this, O man, that judgest them which do such things, and doest the same, that thou shalt escape the judgment of God? (Rom. 2:3).

Don't judge others, and don't fight people who judge you. Leave them to God to take care of. It's not easy to do, but it's the only way. A highly respected man of God once told me, "Remember, if you defend yourself, God can't defend you."

THE GOODNESS OF GOD

> Or despisest thou the riches of his goodness and forbearance and longsuffering; not knowing that the goodness of God leadeth thee to repentance? (Rom. 2:4).

I think we need to change our approach to the Gospel message. Instead of condemning people to hell all the time, preaching a message of condemnation, we ought to tell people how good God is. Did you ever notice how a lot of the churches that are preaching that same old message of *hellfire and brimstone, condemnation, faith doesn't work,* and that *confession is an erroneous New Age message,* are almost empty on Sunday mornings?

People are tired of evil and pain in their lives and are looking for something good for a change. We need to tell them how good our God is, that He is a God of love, and that He loves them and wants to help them in this world and take them to heaven to be with Him in the next.

ASK, SEEK, KNOCK.

> Ask, and it shall be given you; seek, and ye shall find; knock, and it shall be opened unto you: For every one that asketh receiveth; and he that seeketh findeth; and to him that knocketh it shall be opened (Matt. 7:7-8).

God promises that if you will knock, He will open the door. His answers will come.

Everyone who asks receives—everyone! Everyone who seeks finds—everyone!. Everyone who knocks on the door will find it swinging open—everyone!. One of the reasons why some people never get things they want is they don't ask. They don't seek. They don't knock. It's that simple.

Notice what Jesus says next to further assure us of our Father's love:

> Or what man is there of you, whom if his son ask bread, will he give him a stone? Or if he ask a fish,

will he give him a serpent? If ye then, being evil, know how to give good gifts unto your children, how much more shall your Father which is in heaven give good things to them that ask him? (Matt. 7:9-11).

Most parents want to give good gifts to their children: a good education, toys, clothing, etc. You want to give your children things you didn't have. You want their lives to be better than yours was. Your heart tells you to give these things to your children. You have a heart that is going to give *GOOD GIFTS!* That's why you save and work and sacrifice for your children. If that's so about us, how do we dare to have any thoughts that our heavenly Father is less loving and willing than we are?

> If ye then, being evil, know how to give good gifts unto your children, how much more shall your Father which is in heaven give good things to them that ask him? (Matt. 7:11).

If your heavenly Father gives good gifts to you, then how much should you be giving good gifts to others? Jesus said that much was required of those who have been given much. How can we give good things to others, how can we love others, how can we be what God has called us to be, if we do not believe that the God we serve is the God who gives good gifts to us?

For too long our church songs have contained many harmful messages: "Woe is me. I am poor, lonely, depressed. I am on my way to heaven, though." Many of these hymns have to do with how tough life is, how evil and how bad it is to live in this world. I've heard earnest people give testimonies that say, "Oh, pray for me that I will be able to hold on to the end."

Sometimes people are afraid to ask God for good things, because they don't know what His reaction will be. This comes out of what they've learned from religion. Religion may have taught them that God is mad at us.

If we know who God is, what He has, what He can do and what He wants to do for us, then we will know who we are, what we have and what we can do. Likewise, we will know what the devil does not have, does not know and what he cannot do!

It is appropriate to close this chapter with the following affirmation of faith:

I reject anything in my thinking that hinders me from thinking correctly about my heavenly Father. Today, I will fill my mind with good thoughts, thoughts of goodness, forbearance, mercy, grace and love that my heavenly Father is giving to me. Today, right now, I choose to walk in the goodness of God in my life. Enough is enough. Devil, I remind you that I am a child of the living God. I know, in the natural, that if earthly fathers give good things to their children, how much more will my heavenly Father give good things to me because I ask and because I live a godly life. I seek first the Kingdom of God. I expect all things to be added to me in Jesus' name.

God is a giver, not a taker!

In good times and in tough times, our good God will give to us all that we need to make it through this life—abundantly!

9

Who Is God To You?

In All Thy Ways

> Trust in the Lord with all thine heart; and lean not
> unto thine own understanding. In all thy ways
> acknowledge him, and he shall direct thy paths. Be not
> wise in thine own eyes: fear the Lord, and depart from
> evil. It shall be health to thy navel, and marrow to thy
> bones (Prov. 3:5-8).

Don't let your own understanding rob you of what
God intends in your life, and don't serve God half-
heartedly—give Him all of your heart. You can't have
one foot in the world and one foot in the kingdom of God.

"In all thy ways acknowledge him," means with ALL
your heart and ALL your ways acknowledge Him, and
He will direct ALL your path. To receive direction from
God for every part of your life, He must have every part
of your life. Many of us want God involved in our life
in tough times, but too often leave God out of our lives

at other times. Somehow we know that if we get Him involved in our lives, He might not let us get involved in what we want to get involved in—so we try to leave Him out of selected areas. Some people never reach their destiny, their place and position in God because they don't acknowledge God in all their ways.

"Be not wise in thine own eyes [Don't try to plan this thing out for yourself.]; fear the LORD, and depart from evil." "Depart from evil" means leave it alone, run from it. (Notice in all of these the emphasis on the importance of making a personal choice, and what happens when we make the right choice.)

"It shall be health to thy navel" The word "health" in Hebrew actually means "medicine." It will be medicine to you. The word "navel refers to the umbilical cord— the tie of life. It's the vital link that transfers life itself from a mother to a child. It will be medicine, health and life to you.

"And marrow [moisture], to thy bones." It shall be moisture to your bones. You will not get arthritis. You will not get all tensed up. Your blood will be healthy. The Scriptures often speak of dry bones, which are a type of spiritual death. This passage gives the opposite picture— marrow, life, moisture and health for our bones.

When your relationship with God is what it's supposed to be, you won't have to keep confessing health, prosperity, goodness and blessings because they'll automatically happen to you.

GIVING AND RECEIVING

Honour the LORD with thy substance, and with
the firstfruits of all thine increase: So shall thy barns

be filled with plenty, and thy presses shall burst out
with new wine (Prov. 3:9-10).

Many times in the Scriptures it tells us that God's
promises to materially bless us are dependent on our
giving. "Honour the LORD . . . with the firstfruits of all
thine increase" refers to tithing. Firstfruits are tithes (see
Lev. 23:10 and Ezek. 44:30). When you tithe, your barns
will be full and your presses will break forth with new
wine. What a glorious promise that is!

The Bible is a gift book. God wants to bless His
people with every good gift. Notice what He says in the
Book of Deuteronomy:

Then will the LORD drive out all these nations
from before you, and ye shall possess greater nations
and mightier than yourselves (Deut. 11:23).

When you're the underdog and you still come out on
top, you know God's on your side. That's when you know
it is God who's moving on your behalf. He moves in and
expands your horizons, enabling you to reclaim lost
territory.

Every place whereon the soles of your feet shall
tread shall be yours: from the wilderness and Lebanon,
from the river, the river Euphrates, even unto the
uttermost sea shall your coast be (Deut. 11:24).

In other words, from north to south, from east to west,
wherever you put your feet, you'll be able to take
dominion. God wants to bless you in every way. You'll
become a victor, a winner, a tough person in tough times
because your God is good.

115

> There shall no man be able to stand before you:
> for the LORD your God shall lay the fear of you and
> the dread of you upon all the land that ye shall tread
> upon, as he hath said unto you (Deut. 11:25).

God always goes back to His covenant. He keeps His Word. As Solomon pointed out, there is nothing new under the sun. The faith message wasn't created in 1974 in Tulsa, when Rhema Bible School was born. Faith, divine healing, prosperity and all the rest of God's wonderful blessings have been His plan for His people from Genesis 1 when He made man in His own image and likeness, and told man to take dominion and authority, right on through today and beyond. He said to subdue, conquer and take the earth, because it's ours. God has never altered His plan from "day one." It's His plan for you! "Behold, I set before you this day a blessing and a curse" (Deut. 11:26).

Every Christian should be blessed by God. The Scripture, however, says that we make the choice as to whether we'll be blessed or cursed. People will often say, "If it's God's will." There's no question about God's will. His Word reveals the whole counsel of God. It's His will for us to be blessed, not cursed.

The blessings of God are conditional, however. The condition is obedience. We'll receive a blessing *if* we obey ". . . the commandments of the LORD your God, which I command you this day" (Deut. 11:27). God won't do anything for you if you're in disobedience— for example, when you haven't honored the Lord with your substance and the firstfruit of your increase.

God clearly states that He will bless us if we obey

Him. Deuteronomy 11:27 is obviously not only talking about tithing, it's talking about everything in life. You can't live an unholy life and go to a holy God and expect Him to bless you. You can't cheat people, lie to them, steal from them, deceive them, talk about them, live in sin and then go to the house of God and shout a little bit, do a little dance and say, "Hallelujah, I'm being blessed!" That's not being blessed, that's bringing "strange fire before God" (Lev. 10:1).

GOD'S PLAN

God's plan is to bless you—if you obey Him. It's more costly to disobey than it is to obey. "Trust and obey, for there's no other way."

All you have to do is obey. You don't even have to rebuke the devil over your finances. God said that if we bring our tithes into the storehouse, He will rebuke the devourer for our sakes (Mal. 3:11). We spend too much time rebuking the devil: "I bind you, I bind you, I curse you." Chill out! The key is obedience. Just obey, and God starts doing it all for you.

Isaiah wrote of the coming of John the Baptist, and how the desert would become a highway for God:

> The voice of him that crieth in the wilderness,
> Prepare ye the way of the LORD, make straight in the
> desert a highway for our God (Isa. 40:3).

You know miracles are happening when the desert becomes useful and fruitful. I hear people say all the time, "I'm in a dry place." No place is drier than the desert. Arid places become useful, fruitful and blessed when God shows up.

> Every valley shall be exalted, and every mountain and hill shall be made low: and the crooked shall be made straight, and the rough places plain (Isa. 40:4).

God is in the valleys. He lifts us up when we're in the valleys of life. We don't have to fear evil when we're in the valleys because God is with us. And that mountain of difficulty in your path, that hill that you cannot get over, will be leveled by the power of God. God says He'll blast it to nothing on your behalf!

Have you ever been on a crooked path? You feel as if you're going somewhere, but you never get there, and when you turn a corner there's a longer road still ahead. It can almost seem as if you missed your turn and lost your way. But the Scripture says your way will be made straight and your rough places made plain. God will also take the bumps out of your highway and give you a smooth trip.

Obey God and your desert places will become fruitful, your valleys will be exalted, your mountains will be cut down, your crooked paths will be made straight, and your rough roads will be made smooth. God will settle all your troubled ways when you obey Him. Nothing is too hard for God. He can do anything but fail. He specializes in "things thought impossible."

DREAM YOUR WAY TO VICTORY

Some people never reach their destiny in God because they don't have a dream. They don't acknowledge God in all their ways and so He doesn't direct their paths. But, if God is directing your path, you become a dreamer. God has a plan to save the whole world, and this becomes your vision as well.

Some people let their cultures hold them back, others their lack of education. They fail to realize that some of the greatest people in the world, who have done major things for God and for the human race, were from disadvantaged cultures and had little education. Neither culture background nor education is the issue—having a dream and a vision is. God says, "Where there is no vision, the people perish . . ." (Prov. 29:18). God is looking for people who'll say, "I believe, no matter what!" Believers like that won't allow the circumstances of life to deflect, deter, disappoint, or discourage them from reaching the place in God that He has for them.

CHOICES OF LIFE

We choose what we believe. We choose our dreams and our visions—and our blessings. How we chose to respond to the situations of life determines whether God helps us with those situations. For example, if we choose to be crooked with the government and not pay our taxes, God won't bless our finances. We must not lie about our earnings or about anything else. Our lies about anything turn God away from helping us. A holy God will never help a liar.

When curses come upon us, is it God who brings the curses? No, absolutely not. If you disobey God, His protection lifts from your life and the serpent comes and bites. God doesn't bring the curse, you bring it by

119

disobeying God and causing His protection to lift. When that happens, the enemy gains an entrance into your life. The choice is yours—blessings or curses (Deut. 30:19).

EQUALITY IN CHRIST

> For ye are all the children of God by faith in Christ Jesus. For as many of you as have been baptized into Christ [By the Spirit into the body of Christ, being regenerated, born again] have put on Christ. There is neither Jew nor Greek, there is neither bond nor free, there is neither male nor female: for ye are all one in Christ Jesus (Gal. 3:26-28).

No matter what your nationality, color, sex, physical ability or condition, background, economy, or education—find your place in God! God has a plan and purpose for you—a specific plan and a specific purpose that is based upon His love, and only His love, for you!

All our social problems would be solved if we stopped using human wisdom and simply became everything God wants us to be. When true communication between us and God becomes a reality, then true communication between Christians can become a reality. We are one in Christ—no walls should divide those who are in Him.

LITTLE IS MUCH WHEN GOD IS IN IT

We constantly need to remind ourselves not to look at things the way the world looks at them. The network news, the stock market report, the talk shows, the newspapers and all the other sources of worldly information give only a small part of the total picture. They give us a negative point of view.

But what happens when God gets involved? The widow woman in First Kings 17 was making her last pancake. She had a few sticks, a handful of meal and a little oil left in the barrel. She and her son were going to have their last feast and get ready to die. They were in the midst of a terrible famine. But, all of a sudden, Elijah the prophet shows up and tells her to make him a cake. Naturally, the widow protested,

> And Elijah said unto her, Fear not; go and do as thou hast said: but make me thereof a little cake first, and bring it unto me, and after make for thee and for thy son (1 Kings 17:13).

She did what he said, and the result was that her little oil and handful of meal lasted all through the famine— enough for her, her son, and Elijah. God can change a circumstance before you can even realize what's happening, or what He's doing.

Some fishermen went fishing all night and caught nothing, and came in to shore to wash their nets. Jesus showed up and asked one of them named Simon if He could preach from his ship. After he finished, ". . . he said unto Simon, Launch out into the deep, and let down your nets for a draught" (Luke 5:4).

You can imagine what Simon must have thought at first: "We're experienced fishermen, and he's nothing but an itinerant preacher and he thinks he can tell us how to catch fish!"

But something about Jesus made them do what He said, and when they did,

> . . . they inclosed a great multitude of fishes: and
> their net brake. And they beckoned unto their partners,
> which were in the other ship, that they should come
> and help them. And they came, and filled both the
> ships, so that they began to sink (Luke 5:6-7).

Another time, the men who collected the tribute money (taxes) came to the Lord's disciple, Peter and said, "Doth not your master pay tribute?" (Matt. 17:24) In other words, does he pay or does he cheat? Apparently there was no money in the common purse that day to pay the taxes with, so Jesus said to Peter,

> . . . go thou to the sea, and cast an hook, and take
> up the fish that first cometh up; and when thou hast
> opened his mouth, thou shalt find a piece of money:
> that take, and give unto them for me and thee (Matt.
> 17:27).

And here we are worrying, "The economy is bad. Washington is bad. The dollar is shrinking. What am I going to do?" We act as if God could no longer do miracles as He did in the days when His Son walked the earth.

BLESSINGS EVERYWHERE

> Blessed shalt thou be in the city, and blessed shalt
> thou be in the field. Blessed shall be the fruit of thy
> body, and the fruit of thy ground, and the fruit of thy
> cattle, the increase of thy kine, and the flocks of thy
> sheep. Blessed shall be thy basket and thy store.
> Blessed shalt thou be when thou comest in, and blessed
> shalt thou be when thou goest out (Deut. 28: 3-6).

122

God didn't say, "You'll be blessed only when the economy is good." There are no qualifications attached to His plan and program for your life. You *will* be blessed.

We need to know how to "daydream with the Holy Ghost." Start seeing yourself as blessed. Start seeing your business as blessed. Start seeing your family as blessed. Start seeing yourself as God sees you. Start seeing blessings everywhere!

Who Your Enemies Are May Surprise You

> Think not that I am come to send peace on earth: I came not to send peace, but a sword. For I am come to set a man at variance against his father, and the daughter against her mother, and the daughter in law against her mother in law And a man's foes shall be they of his own household. He that loveth father or mother more than me is not worthy of me: and he that loveth son or daughter more than me is not worthy of me. And he that taketh not his cross, and followeth after me, is not worthy of me. He that findeth his life shall lose it: and he that loseth his life for my sake shall find it (Matt. 10:34-39).

The first enemy that will keep you from your destiny in God is your family. This may be a surprise to you. But remember, if you have a problem with your family, God can solve it—if everybody wants it solved.

Someone will say, "God breaks up families." No. God loves families. He restores them. However, we need to be realistic about the truth of His Word. Jesus is saying, however, that sometimes your faith in God will cause some of your family members to totally misunderstand you. Some family members may not support you, some may even oppose you.

When you first got saved, you may have gone home and told your wife, husband, children, mother, father or some relative, "I just got saved!"

They may have responded, "Oh, no. You're not one of those Holy Rollers now, are you?"

Maybe at one time you drank with them, played with them, ran with them. Perhaps you had lots of fun and a good relationship with them. You told jokes and did some things you're not proud of now, but they loved you. When you say to them, "I got saved!" it may be interpreted from their side as meaning, "I've lost my best friend," or even that you think you're now morally superior to them.

I've watched similar things happen to husbands and wives and other family relationships. A wife would get saved, go home and tell her husband, and he would get angry. Sometimes he'd even beat his wife in an effort to control her. Sometimes it got to the point where the woman would have to leave her home.

I know men today whose ministries have been hindered and killed because their wives wouldn't pay the price in the early days of ministry when it's rough. They would not, or could not, pay the price and they robbed their husbands of being in the ministry of the Gospel. So all the rest of their lives they're missing God.

I know other people who have never reached their potential in God because they have listened to what their family members thought about them. That's what Jesus was talking about when He said, ". . . A prophet is not

124

without honour, save in his own country, and in his own house" (Matt. 13:57). Family members seldom think that another family member can be somebody used by God for His kingdom. If Christians—especially new ones— pay attention to that kind of negative family attitude toward them, they can even end up denying their birthright in God.

JOSEPH'S ENEMIES

Joseph had a dream from God.

> . . . and he told it his brethren: and they hated him yet the more. And he said unto them, Hear, I pray you, this dream which I have dreamed: For, behold, we were binding sheaves in the field, and, lo, my sheaf arose, and also stood upright; and, behold, your sheaves stood round about, and made obeisance to my sheaf. (Gen. 37:5-7).

Telling his dream to his brothers may not have been the best thing for Joseph to do. Sometimes when God speaks to you, you have to hold on to that word until the right season, or those you tell may react the way Joseph's brothers did.

> And his brethren said to him, Shalt thou indeed reign over us? or shalt thou indeed have dominion over us? And they hated him yet the more for his dreams, and for his words (Gen. 37:8).

They were so angry at Joseph that they threw him into a pit out in the wilderness. Then when some

125

Midianite slavers came along they sold Joseph to them and he ended up in slavery in Egypt. But the dream from God remained within him.

After many more tough times, and many years in prison, God gave Joseph an interpretation of a dream that Pharaoh had, who was so pleased with the accuracy of the interpretation and the warning of the coming famine, that he made Joseph second in command in all of Egypt, second only to Pharaoh himself.

One day when the famine that Joseph had interpreted from the dream became severe all over the face of the earth, Joseph's father, Jacob, heard that there was corn in Egypt and sent Joseph's brothers there to seek help. When they got to the place where Joseph sat, they bowed down before him. Remember Joseph's dream? God always fulfills His promises. His Word never returns to Him void (Isa. 55:11).

Eventually, Joseph revealed his identity to his brothers, for they had not recognized him after all the years that had passed. When he did, they thought he was going to have killed for selling him into slavery, but he told them,

> Now therefore be not grieved, nor angry with yourselves, that ye sold me hither: for God did send me before you to preserve life. For these two years hath the famine been in the land: and yet there are five years, in the which there shall neither be earing nor harvest. And God sent me before you to preserve you a posterity in the earth, and to save your lives by a great deliverance. So now it was not you that sent me hither, but God: and he hath made me a father to Pharaoh, and lord of all his house, and a ruler throughout all the land of Egypt (Gen. 45:5-8).

The people God blesses are never resentful. They are never bitter. They never try to get back at people. God's people are not vengeful. They are forgiving. They are givers. They bless those who oppose them

People with guts and determination, tenacity and toughness, do not give in when the going gets tough. They are not easily discouraged even when their family puts them down. They are looking unto Jesus as the Author and Finisher of their faith, and unto God as the giver of all good gifts.

God has given you a dream and a vision. You cannot reach your destiny in God if you allow the circumstances of life to hold you back. First of all, you have to understand the character of God. He is working in you both to will and to do of His good pleasure (Phil. 2:13). "Faithful is he that calleth you, who also will do it" (1 Thess. 5:24).

See yourself as God sees you, not as others see you. See God as He really is. A real sense of breakthrough will come when you reach your vision, the destination that God has for you. You have so much to look forward to, regardless of your age, your race, your sex, your background, your family, your culture or your educational status.

God has a definite and specific plan and purpose for your life.

And whatever you have need of from God in your life, always remember:

Our God is El Shaddai, the God who is more than enough.

He is Jehovah-Rapha, our healer.

He is Jehovah-Shalom, our peace.

He is Jehovah-Jireh, our provider.

He is Everything to us.

127

10

God's Way Is Perfect

God's way is always best and always perfect. Since our way is never perfect and seldom best, God's way is often contrary to our way, which can be frustrating for us. What God chooses is not always what we like, nor the way we like it. Nevertheless, hold fast—God's plan for your life is good.

PUT ON THE WHOLE ARMOR OF GOD

Finally, my brethren, be strong in the Lord, and in the power of his might. Put on the whole armour of God, that ye may be able to stand against the wiles of the devil. For we wrestle not against flesh and blood, but against principalities, against powers, against the rulers of the darkness of this world, against spiritual wickedness in high places. Wherefore take unto you the whole armour of God, that ye may be able to withstand in the evil day, and having done all, to stand. Stand therefore, having your loins girt about with truth,

and having on the breastplate of righteousness; And
your feet shod with the preparation of the gospel of
peace; Above all, taking the shield of faith, wherewith
ye shall be able to quench all the fiery darts of the
wicked (Eph. 6:10-16).

The Apostle Paul tells us to put on God's armor to
protect ourselves from the devil, who ". . . as a roaring
lion, walketh about, seeking whom he may devour" (1
Pet. 5:8). We're not to fight the enemy in the strength
of our own might. Only the might of God's power can
give us the protection we need to be strong in the Lord.

The word "wiles" in our text-verse means plans and
deceptions of the devil. It's God's armor that protects
us from each of the devil's attempts to get us off track.
One way he does is to make us think that other human
beings—family, friends, enemies, politicians, etc.—are
our enemies. But Paul clearly tells us that our enemies
are not flesh and blood, they're spirits. Always
remember that!

Notice in Paul's admonition that it's *our* responsibility
to put on the whole armor of God and do something
about our problem. It's God's armour, but you have to
put it on—it isn't automatically put on when you get
saved or filled with the Holy Spirit. So you need to do
what Paul says, otherwise when the evil day comes, you
may not be able to withstand it if you're not wearing the
full armor of God.

From Paul's words, we can also see that there will
be times in life when we've done all we can and the evil
still progresses against us. What do we do then? Stand
like a rock and keep standing and let the problem bounce
off God's armour! But "above all," hold forth "the shield

130

of faith!" By so doing, you'll quench ALL the fiery darts of the devil—not just a *few* of them, ALL OF THEM!

FOR A SEASON

> Wherein ye greatly rejoice, though now for a season, if need be, ye are in heaviness through manifold temptations (1 Pet. 1:6).

It has been said, "Tough times don't last, but tough people do." Manifold temptations may come for a season. God gives us the changing seasons of the year to teach us gratitude. "If winter comes, can spring be far behind?" The seasons change. You may be in winter now, but spring is just around the corner. The seasons do change. Stand!

The devil attacks your faith because he doesn't want you to trust God. He doesn't want you to stand on His promises. He doesn't want you to believe God and confess His Word to encourage yourself. He doesn't want you to prosper. He wants your marriage unhappy and your kids on drugs. He wants you discouraged and depressed. So he attacks your faith because that's what you need the most.

JOY UNSPEAKABLE

> That the trial of your faith, being much more precious than of gold that perisheth, though it be tried with fire, [Paul said in Ephesians that the devil was going to throw fiery darts at us] might be found unto praise and honour and glory at the appearing of Jesus Christ: Whom having not seen, ye love; in whom,

131

> though now ye see him not, yet believing, ye rejoice with joy unspeakable and full of glory (1 Pet. 1:7-8).

A revival of joy is coming to the Church. God is taking our attention off what we've been through, and He's putting our attention on what He's going to take us to!

> Of which salvation the prophets have inquired and searched diligently, who prophesied of the grace that should come unto you: searching what, or what manner of time the Spirit of Christ which was in them did signify, when it testified beforehand the sufferings of Christ, and the glory that should follow (1 Pet. 1:10-11).

We must always remember that the sufferings of this present time are not worthy to be compared with the glory that God will reveal in the ages to come.

> Wherefore gird up the loins of your mind, be sober, [Don't act like a drunk, not knowing where you're going or how you're going to get there] and hope to the end for the grace that is to be brought unto you at the revelation of Jesus Christ; As obedient children, not fashioning yourselves according to the former lusts in your ignorance: But as he which hath called you is holy, so be ye holy in all manner of conversation; Because it is written, Be ye holy; for I am holy (1 Pet. 1:13-16).

"Wherefore gird up the loins of your mind...." Faith, through which we quench Satan's fiery darts, works through a strong renewed mind.

God is saying through the Apostle Peter that you can

be what He said you can be, because He's given you the way to become just that. But you're going to have to understand that you need to guard your mind and protect it because Satan is out to rob your faith. So keep a guard on your mind. Put the girdle of truth on your mind, because your faith is being tried. If Satan can get your faith, he can stop you from quenching his fiery darts.

About being holy, Jesus said to the Pharisees, "You whitewashed sepulchers. You are white and clean on the outside, but inside you are full of dead men's bones." They were trusting in the wrong approach to holiness. Holiness comes from the inside. When you get your heart right, then you start living a holy life.

SANCTIFIED POWER

In Exodus 12:15 this is written, "Seven days shall ye eat unleavened bread . . . ." In the Old Testament, "unleavened bread" in the Scriptures refers to holiness, and leaven refers to sin. In this verse, God was telling the Israelites to sanctify themselves in preparation for the Lord's passover and their departure from Egypt.

The Scripture continues: "even the first day ye shall put away leaven out of your houses [God wants sin out of your house]: for whosoever eateth leavened bread from the first day until the seventh day, that soul shall be cut off from Israel" (Exod. 12:15).

This passage show how serious God is about his people not sinning, about their living holy lives. "Seven days shall there be no leaven found in your houses: for whosoever eateth that which is leavened, even that soul shall be cut off from the congregation of Israel, whether

133

he be a stranger, or born in the land" (Exod. 12:19).

God said, in effect, "The only way you can enter into My covenant is if you observe My commandments." Divine protection, divine guidance, divine blessing—these don't just automatically drop out of the sky, they come by obedience to what God tells us to do. And He says to get the sin (leaven) out of you and out of your house.

CLOSE THE DOOR ON THE DEVIL

> Ye shall eat nothing leavened; in all your habitations shall ye eat unleavened bread. Then Moses called for all the elders of Israel, and said unto them, Draw out and take you a lamb according to your families, and kill the passover. And ye shall take a bunch of hyssop, and dip it in the blood that is in the basin, and strike the lintel and the two side posts with the blood that is in the basin and none of you shall go out at the door of his house until the morning (Exod. 12:20-22).

God told them to take no leavened bread for seven days. Seven is the number of perfection. It's God's number. They were to close the door, go inside, roast and eat the lamb. They were to take the blood, dip the hyssop into it, put the blood on the lintel and doorposts of their house, and then go inside and stay there until morning. Then God tells them why they are to do these things:

> For the LORD will pass through to smite the Egyptians; and when he seeth the blood upon the

lintel, and on the two side posts, the LORD will pass over the door, and will not suffer the destroyer to come in unto your houses to smite you (Exod. 12:23).

God told them to get inside the house. Close the door. Shut it tight. Don't come out until morning. Eat the whole Passover Lamb, not just part. Make sure there's enough for your entire family. Sprinkle the blood on the doorposts of your house. If you have the blood outside your house, the Lamb inside you, and your door shut tight—I'll pass over you and won't allow the destroyer to touch you.

In the same way, God says to you today that if you've been born-again, if you've eaten Christ the Passover Lamb—received Him as your Lord and Savior—and have been washed by His blood, and have shut the doors of yourself and your house—your family—tight against sin; that He will bless you and protect you, and not allow the destroyer to touch you or anyone in your house.

Are you saved?

Are you in Christ?

Is Christ in you?

Are you living a holy life?

Are you guarding your family against sin?

That's all that counts.

THE BROKEN HEDGE

God establishes a hedge around his covenant people that is maintained until they sin and break down the hedge themselves by their disobedience. In Psalm 80,

135

Asaph, wrote about this very thing happening: "Why hast thou then broken down her hedges, so that all they which pass by the way do pluck her?" (Ps. 80:12).

In the Book of Job, Satan appears before God in heaven and makes some interesting comments about God's hedge of protection around Job and the blessings that resulted from that hedge:

> Hast not thou made an hedge about him, and about his house, and about all that he hath on every side? thou hast blessed the work of his hands, and his substance is increased in the land (Job 1:10).

David frequently wrote about the blessings of God and His everlasting covenant with Israel. In Psalm 139 he exclaims about the wonder of it all: "Thou hast beset me behind and before, and laid thine hand upon me. Such knowledge is too wonderful for me; it is high, I cannot attain unto it (Psalm 139:5-6).

The New International Version (NIV) translates verse 5 as, "You hemmed me in behind and before." Another translation has it as, "You hedged me in."

Then in Ecclesiastes 10:8, we read about the hedge being broken down and what happens when it is: "He that diggeth a pit shall fall into it; and whoso breaketh an hedge, a serpent shall bite him". The serpent is the evil one. He will bite the one who breaks the hedge of protection. If we're the ones who break the hedge down from around ourselves, then why do we blame God every time we have a problem? Why do we act as if it's His fault?

This verse says if a man digs a pit, he'll fall into it. If he breaks the hedge, a serpent will bite him. This shows us that God didn't break the hedge around Job. Job had something to do with the hedge of protection around his family being broken. Look at that verse from Ecclesiastes again: "He that diggeth a pit shall fall into it [It doesn't say God dug the pit and pushed you in]; and whoso breaketh an hedge, a serpent shall bite him." [This doesn't say God took the hedge down or was the one who hurt you].

THE FENCED VINEYARD

> Now will I sing to my wellbeloved a song of my beloved touching his vineyard. [His vineyard then was Israel, but now is the Body of Christ.] My wellbeloved hath a vineyard in a very fruitful hill: And he fenced it . . . (Isa. 5:1-2).

God built a fence around His well-beloved in a very fruitful hill. What kind of fence would this be? It would certainly not be a little picket fence.

> . . . and gathered out the stones thereof, and planted it with the choicest vine, and built a tower in the midst of it, and also made a winepress therein: and he looked that it should bring forth grapes, and it brought forth wild grapes (Isa. 5:2).

What did God do for this vineyard?

- He fenced it.
- He took the stones out.
- He planted it with the choicest vine.
- He built a tower to watch and guard it.

137

• He made a wine press because He expected good grapes.

But, instead, look what happened:

> And now, O inhabitants of Jerusalem, and men of Judah, judge, I pray you, betwixt me and my vineyard. What could have been done more to my vineyard, that I have not done in it? wherefore, *when I looked that it should bring forth good grapes, brought it forth wild grapes?* And now go to; I will tell you what I will do to my vineyard: I will take away the hedge thereon, and it shall be eaten up; and break down the wall thereof, and it shall be trodden down" (Isa. 5:3-5, italics mine).

It wasn't God who took away their hedge, it was their disobedience that took it away. God had no choice but to respond accordingly. God planted the choicest vine (Israel), He fenced it, He gathered out the stones, He built a tower and He made a winepress. But the grapes (fruit) that Israel brought forth were wild (disobedient). They did not obey God, and He had no choice. You can see Israel's disobedience in several places in chapter 5, and in verses 13 and 14 the consequences of their disobeying God and breaking down His hedge of protection.

> . . . because they have no knowledge: and their honourable men are famished, and their multitude dried up with thirst. Therefore hell (Sheol) hath enlarged herself, and opened her mouth without measure: and their glory, and their multitude, and their pomp, and he that rejoiceth, shall descend into it.

138

God did everything needed to plant a good vineyard that would produce good grapes, even to putting a wall of protection around it—all that was needed was to obey Him and develop and produce good fruit. But His vineyard, Israel, would not obey Him and so produced only the wild, evil, fruit that comes from disobeying a holy God. So God said to them about His vineyard, about Israel,

> And I will lay it waste: it shall not be pruned, nor digged; but there shall come up briers and thorns: I will also command the clouds that they rain no rain upon it. For the vineyard of the LORD of hosts is the house of Israel, and the men of Judah his pleasant plant: and he looked for judgment, but behold oppression; for righteousness, but behold a cry (Isa. 5:6-7).

Joshua said, ". . . As for me and my house, we will serve the Lord" (Josh. 24:15). I want God's blessing on my house and on me! I'm not going to walk in the curse. I'm not going to have God say, "O.K., clouds, no rain on his seed."

All you have to do is to cooperate with God.

He wants to lift that snare out of your life.

The devil, who has oppressed you and harassed you and disturbed you, and tried to get you off track, will be defeated.

God is waited for your obedience and faith so He can boot Satan out of your way.

God is always a good God to tough, obedient, faith people when they're in tough times—and all His ways are perfect!

139

As for God, his way is perfect: the word of the LORD is tried: he is a buckler, a mighty buckler, to all those that trust in him (Ps. 18:30).

11

Friendship With God

Abraham was called, "the friend of God" (James 2:23). Was he called the friend of God because he was a sinless man? No, he made mistakes just like the rest of us.

God spoke to Abram (later Abraham) and told him to leave his relatives, leave his house, leave his home and go where He told him to—and Abram obeyed (Gen. 12:1). He tried to obey everything God asked him to do. He made some mistakes, but he held on to his relationship with God. Abraham met God as Jehovah-Jireh, the Provider, when he was preparing to offer up his only son. Abraham ascended the mountain to sacrifice Isaac and just as he was ready to plunge the knife into his son,

> . . . the angel of the LORD called unto him out of heaven, and said, Abraham, Abraham: and he said, Here am I. And he said, Lay not thine hand upon the lad, neither do thou any thing unto him: for now I know that thou fearest God, seeing thou hast not

withheld thy son, thine only son from me. And Abraham lifted up his eyes, and looked, and behold behind him a ram caught in a thicket by his horns: and Abraham went and took the ram, and offered him up for a burnt offering in the stead of his son. And Abraham called the name of that place Jehovahjireh [the Lord will provide]: as it is said to this day, In the mount of the LORD it shall be seen [provided] (Gen. 22:11-14).

Abraham was a friend of God. That's why God blessed Abraham. Jesus told His disciples that if they wanted to be His friends, then they would have to do some things for Him—"Ye are my friends, if ye do whatsoever I command you" (John 15:14).

Friendship is a mutual participation in a covenant relationship. If you and I are supposed to be friends and you are looking at what you can get from me, or if I'm looking at what I can get from you, we are not true friends. In fact, we are bad for each other. Such a relationship is one of co-dependency—a relationship based upon what each person can get from the other that fulfills some need. In a co-dependency relationship, both people are takers, and may not be capable of forming a true friendship.

God, however, isn't looking for takers, He's looking for givers. He wants faithful friends, those who are friends for the sake of the other person. When it comes to God, He wants ALL of your friendship, not just part of it. He won't accept a partial friendship, one that is split between Him and something else, especially something of the world.

> Ye adulterers and adulteresses, know ye not that the friendship of the world is enmity with God? whosoever therefore will be a friend of the world is the enemy of God (James 4:4).

God is opposed to all forms of adultery, both physical and spiritual. The principle He is putting forth here is, if you disobey Him and His commandments because you want to be friends with the world, you cannot be His friend. It's spiritual adultery when we turn from friendship with God and become friends with the world. To do so makes us the enemy of God. He will have no other gods before Him.

God is clearly saying that if you associate with the world's system so much that the world's system controls the way you think and act, you cannot be His friend. Sometimes our friendship with certain people stands in the way of our friendship with God.

Anyone who dishonors God cannot be your close friend if you want to serve God and serve Him in the right way. This does not mean that we treat people in the world rudely, but it does mean that we can't have a close friendship with them. This is especially important for single people who are looking for a mate. Don't look for one in the world.

"Well, I can't find anyone in church!"

The trouble with that kind of thinking is that you're trying to find your mate instead of allowing God to find the right one for you. "But, how long am I going to have to wait?" Until you get right with God! Who wants to marry someone who's confused and searching? That person doesn't really know what he or she wants. "But

I'm running out of patience!" It's better to run out of patience than to run into a bad marriage.

COME OUT FROM AMONG THEM

We can't expect God to be intimate and close to us when we've adapted a style and way of living that conforms to the world. Paul wrote, ". . . Come out from among them, and be ye separate, saith the Lord . . ." (2 Cor. 6:17). This doesn't mean that we have to move to the mountains and live like a hermit. It simply means that we shouldn't become so entangled with the yoke of the world's bondage that the world dictates what we should believe, how we should act, where we should go, what we should say or how we should live.

Over the years, I've watched young people who were strong in God meet someone and fall in love. Then, all of a sudden, their desire and love toward God is turned toward another human being. You must never leave the Source of what made you into the person you are. Relationships should enhance your life, not detract from it.

One reason some people can't find a mate is that they're looking for someone just like themselves. They feel that there's safety in someone just like themselves. They reason that this will help them understand the other person better and thereby relate to him or her. We don't always stop to realize that God, however, may be bringing someone into our lives who is different from us—that He may want to do so to correct us in certain areas of weakness in our lives.

A friend is someone who can correct you when you're wrong, and can receive correction when he is

144

wrong without becoming offended. Most of us want to hang around people who never challenge who we are or how we act. Such people never challenge the way we talk, the way we think, the things we do. This kind of person is not a true friend. We feel more comfortable with someone who always agrees with us. We would rather have no confrontation and remain the same, rather than meet someone who will tell us, "Whoa, wait a minute! You need to get your life in order!"

In light of these principles, it stands to reason that we should start thinking, "My new friends must come from the body of Christ." Once that's established in your thinking, it becomes a general principle in establishing friendships.

Search for friends among those who are strong in God, who display God's love and maintain a strong relationship with God. If they can please God, they certainly should be able to please you! Most of our human searching is based on looks. Physical attractiveness is so important to people today! This goes beyond choosing husbands and wives, boy friends and girl friends, and affects our relationships in general. We want our friends to be good-looking because this enhances our position, prestige and influence. Attractiveness is a highly prized and desirable commodity in the world today, and to our shame we have brought that same carnal attitude into the Church. As the world goes, so goes the Church!

MAN-PLEASER OR GOD-PLEASER?

In his epistle to the Galatians, Paul is chastising Gentiles who have been saved but are now being influenced by Judaizers, who have come in and brought division. They have split the people, and they have split the Word of God apart, by saying that God's people needed to go back into form, ritual and religion. They taught that you could be saved only by Christ plus circumcision, and that they needed to keep the traditional holy days, etc.

Paul tells them:

> I marvel that ye are so soon removed from him that called you into the grace of Christ unto another gospel: Which is not another; but there be some that trouble you, and would pervert the gospel of Christ. But though we, or an angel from heaven, preach any other gospel unto you than that which we have preached unto you, let him be accursed. As we said before, so say I now again, if any man preach any other gospel unto you than that ye have received, let him be accursed (Gal. 1:6-9).

The punishment that is reserved for anyone who tries to pervert the Gospel of Jesus Christ is that a curse would be placed upon them. The word "accursed" shows how strongly God feels about this.

Paul then tells them, "For do I now persuade men, or God? or do I seek to please men? For if I yet pleased men, I should not be the servant of Christ" (Gal. 1:10). The servant (or friend) of Christ is someone who seeks to please Him at all times. There was never a better or more faithful friend of Christ than the Apostle Paul.

Later, Paul got himself into trouble when he went to the council at Jerusalem and confronted the religious Judiazers for trying to bring to bear the law upon his Gentile converts by going to them and teaching that to be saved they had to be circumcised and observe all the Jewish rituals. This incensed Paul and Barnabas, the prophet and teacher who traveled with him for awhile:

> And certain men which came down from Judaea taught the brethren, and said, Except ye be circumcised after the manner of Moses, ye cannot be saved. When therefore Paul and Barnabas had no small dissension and disputation with them, they determined that Paul and Barnabas, and certain other of them, should go up to Jerusalem unto the apostles and elders about this question (Acts 15:1-2).

Paul wasn't afraid of them, regardless of what standing they seemed to have in the Church. He refused to fall into a performance-oriented approach that would make him try to comply with their expectations. He had the courage of his convictions, and he spoke to them forthrightly. Will you do the same when people challenge you because of your faith, and criticize your beliefs? Will you be a God-pleaser or a man-pleaser?

Don't take this lightly. Every one of us likes to be liked. Someone might say, "I don't care what anybody thinks about me." If they say that, they probably aren't telling the truth. Everybody wants others to think good about them. The question is, how far do you carry this perceived need? You can carry it so far that you're no longer a friend of God. If you're not a friend of God, then you're a friend of the world, and in God's eyes that's spiritual adultery.

BE A COMMITTED CHRISTIAN

> And they came again to Jerusalem: and as he was walking in the temple, there come to him the chief priests, and the scribes, and the elders, And say unto him, By what authority doest thou these things? and who gave thee this authority to do these things? And Jesus answered and said unto them, I will also ask of you one question, and answer me, and I will tell you by what authority I do these things. The baptism of John, was it from heaven, or of men? answer me. And they reasoned with themselves, saying, If we shall say, From heaven; he will say, Why then did ye not believe him? But if we shall say, Of men; they feared the people: for all men counted John, that he was a prophet indeed. And they answered and said unto Jesus, We cannot tell . . . (Mark 11:27-33).

These people were so concerned about what other people might think that they denied their convictions, their faith, their values out of fear of a loss of approval. What they knew, what they said and what they believed, they would not commit to because they were afraid of who they might offend.

What a tragedy in a person's life—to exchange the approval of God for the approval of men. The Scripture tells us, ". . . Let your yea be yea; and your nay, nay" (James 5:12). We all need to be committed to something.

"Well, I don't get any encouragement," someone might remark. You don't need encouragement from people to get plugged into God. Certainly it helps to have someone encourage you, but it's not necessary.

"Well, I've lost my joy."

My answer to such a person, "Well, find it!"

Jesus answered the people-pleasers this way: "Neither do I tell you by what authority I do these things" (Mark 11:33). He was telling them He didn't owe them an explanation. He didn't owe them anything. Popular opinion had changed their answer and had made them say something they did not want to say, and they were afraid to commit to what they knew was right.

We see examples of this in the case of Pilate and Herod when Jesus was accused of fermenting rebellion against Caesar and was brought before them.

> And the whole multitude of them arose, and led him unto Pilate. And they began to accuse him, saying, We found this fellow perverting the nation, and forbidding to give tribute to Caesar, saying that he himself is Christ a King. [Remember, Jesus never said that.] And Pilate asked him, saying, Art thou the King of the Jews? And he answered him and said, Thou sayest it. Then said Pilate to the chief priests and to the people, I find no fault in this man. And they were the more fierce, saying, He stirreth up the people, teaching throughout all Jewry, beginning from Galilee to this place. When Pilate heard of Galilee, he asked whether the man were a Galilaean. And as soon as he knew that he belonged unto Herod's jurisdiction, he sent him to Herod, who himself also was at Jerusalem at that time (Luke 23:1-7).

This is what is known as "passing the buck." What happened with Pilate? What did he do? What did he say? He said, "I find no fault in this man." He had heard them say He was from Galilee and he passed the buck. "Oh, He's a Galilean? That's what I thought. That's exactly

149

what I thought. He has to go to Herod."

> And when Herod saw Jesus, he was exceeding glad: for he was desirous to see him of a long season, because he had heard many things of him; and he hoped to have seen some miracle done by him (Luke 23:8).

When the original Greek says that he was exceeding glad, it implies that he was as happy as if he was seeing someone he had been waiting to see all his life. Has there ever been someone in your life who, when you saw them, your heart beat quickly, your palms sweated and your knees shook? That's exactly what this term connotes. That is how glad Herod was to see Jesus.

Herod was experiencing faith rising up within him. Faith comes by hearing and he heard about the Miracle-worker! He must have thought, "The Miracle Man is coming here. He's coming to Jerusalem, and I'm going to see him!" He had desired to see Jesus for a long time, and I'm certain he was thinking, "Maybe He will do a miracle for me." This public official could have changed world history, but he caved in to public opinion.

> Then he questioned with him in many words; but he answered him nothing. And the chief priests and scribes stood and vehemently accused him. And Herod with his men of war set him at nought, and mocked him, and arrayed him in a gorgeous robe, and sent him again to Pilate. And the same day Pilate and Herod were made friends together: for before they were at enmity between themselves (Luke 23:9-12).

Two guys who had hated each other previously, who

had been at war and enmity with one another, who had been divided over their governing nations and their powers—all of a sudden become friends! Herod, who had been anticipating seeing the Miracle Worker became so easily influenced by his friends and by the world, that he even lowered himself to become the friend of a man he could not stand.

JOB'S COMFORTING FRIENDS

From the Book of Job we know how friends can affect a person negatively. Job's comforters, with seeming good intentions, tried to dissuade Job from pursuing God's goals for his life.

Job's friends came to see him.. He was out of sorts with himself and he started to accuse God of bringing tragedy on him. Then his friends arrived. They sat down by him, and began to tell him, in so many words, "Here is why you got what you did, Job!" His friends began to make insinuations and bring accusations against Job.

"We knew you were evil," they implied.

These men never had as much wealth as Job had. When he fell, they as much as told him, "We knew you got what you did because you were wrong!" They accused him. One of them so much as said, "Tell me your secret sin."

These guys were "fair-weather friends." When I'm down, I don't need someone to kick me. No one has to tell me when I'm down; I know it by myself. That's why I have such a hard time with preachers who try to make people feel so low. They're angry and insulting, "You dirty old sinner. You need to get saved!"

A sinner knows he's in sin. They don't need someone to tell them they're dirty. They need someone to tell them, "I have a message for you. Jesus loves you. God sent His Son to die for you. Let Him give you life!"

Job's friends came to him and kept on accusing him. The Bible says that when Job prayed for his friends, the curse lifted from him. The man was so insulted by his friends that he built up real animosity toward them. Before God could release the blessing on his life, Job had to forgive his would-be friends. In spite of what they had done to Job, God was withholding the blessing from him because Job was holding animosity toward his friends.

If Job had listened to those three "turkeys," he would have never been doubly blessed in the end. Nothing would have ever been restored to him! Finally, Job put his friends in their place. He as much as told them, "Look, what's going on with me is between me and God. Stay out of it."

In the same way, you and I have to be determined that no one will ever deter us from the vision God has placed within us. Sometimes God will give you a vision and people will start talking you out of it. They will tell you, "You can't," "You won't," "It's not possible. It won't work!" Everyone wants to offer you advice—usually bad and usually negative.

Your place in God is not determined by what people think about you. Don't be swayed by public opinion. Don't be like Pilate and Herod. You have to have a heart like Job, who listened, who heard and who finally threw up his hands and told his friends that enough was enough! Be like Job who said, ". . . I know that my redeemer liveth, and that He shall stand in the last day" (Job 19:25).

You have to be determined to hear the voice of God and not permit people to turn you away. If you have a vision, run with it. Don't let discouragement and situations and people stop you and hinder you.

You have to be committed to God. On your way to that vision or destiny, watch what's going on around you. Walk circumspectly and redeem the time.

Micah said that he had friends, but when he had a problem, he went to God. Friends are wonderful, of course, and they are important, but the greatest friend that you can have is God.

12

The Principle of Multiplied Blessings

Two of the greatest earthly blessings that God provides for us are the blessings of physical healing and prosperity, but they have some provisions attached to them. In the Book of Second Kings, there is recorded the story of how Naaman the leper was cleansed by being obedient to the commandment of the prophet Elisha who told him to dip himself in the Jordan River. Gehazi, Elisha's servant, is also mentioned in this passage:

> But Gehazi, the servant of Elisha the man of God, said, Behold, my master hath spared Naaman this Syrian, in not receiving at his hands that which he brought . . . (2 Kings 5:20).

Naaman had brought money and gifts, but Elisha wouldn't accept them. Elisha wasn't too humble to receive the gifts, he was trying to teach these men that they couldn't pay for miracles.

It greatly disturbs me when I hear preachers and prophets saying, "Come to my meeting and sow a thousand-dollar seed, and we will speak the Word of the Lord over you." Anyone who goes to such a meeting isn't operating with a full deck. All chicanery and side-show hype of this sort must be removed from the kingdom of God!

Elisha could have profited from this miracle, but he knew that it would have been wrong to do so. But his servant, Gehazi, must have said to himself something like, "Boy, I don't want Naaman to go back to his house with those gifts. If Elisha doesn't want them, I'll take them."

> . . . but, as the LORD liveth, I will run after him, and take somewhat of him. So Gehazi followed after Naaman. And when Naaman saw him running after him, he lighted down from the chariot to meet him, and said, Is all well? And he said, All is well. My master hath sent me, saying, Behold, even now there be come to me from mount Ephraim two young men of the sons of the prophets: give them, I pray thee, a talent of silver, and two changes of garments (2 Kings 5:20-22).

A talent of silver amounts to approximately $2,000.00 in today's standards.

> And Naaman said, Be content, take two talents. And he urged him, and bound two talents of silver in two bags, with two changes of garments, and laid them upon two of his servants; and they bare them before him. And when he came to the tower, he took them

from their hand, and bestowed them in the house: and he let the men go, and they departed (2 Kings 5:23-24).

In other words, Gehazi took the money from Naaman, hid it in the house and wasn't going to tell Elisha.

But he went in, and stood before his master. And Elisha said unto him, Whence comest thou, Gehazi? And he said, Thy servant went no whither. And he said unto him, Went not mine heart [spirit] with thee, when the man turned again from his chariot to meet thee? (2 Kings 5:25-26).

Through the gift of the word of knowledge, Elisha knew it all. This gift of supernatural knowledge is going to occur increasingly in the Body of Christ as time goes on. The secret schemes and plans are going to be revealed by the Spirit of God, and dishonesty, lying and undermining will be exposed.

. . . Is it a time to receive money, and to receive garments, and oliveyards, and vineyards, and sheep, and oxen, and menservants, and maidservants? (2 Kings 5:26).

Elisha carefully lists the things that Gehazi must have had in his heart. He was going to collect the money and buy some property, animals, a farm, clothing and other things as well. His treasure was on earth, not in heaven.

The leprosy therefore of Naaman shall cleave unto thee, and unto thy seed for ever. And he went out from his presence a leper as white as snow (2 Kings 5:27)

Leprosy—the most dreaded disease of his day— would be Gehazi's reminder of his sin for the rest of his life. People often pursue the right thing for the wrong motives. If your goal in life is to prosper and be in health only so you can have and enjoy earthly things, then your pursuit will lead you to failure in one way or another. You might not get leprosy, but the blessing of God will never be found in your life.

That's why we all need to have a right mind about the things of God. We need to think properly about the multiplied blessings of God and what God wants us to pursue in our lives. We need to pursue God's goals with the right motive and attitude. Jesus said, "But seek ye first the kingdom of God, and his righteousness; and all these things shall be added unto you" (Matt. 6:33).

Jesus is talking about food, clothing, houses— whatever you need in the natural realm—these will be provided for you, if you seek the kingdom of God first. This is not referring to supernatural provision in the sense of a blessing that will overtake you. It is simply talking about natural provision. You and I should not have to pray about our daily needs. We should not have to confess the Word over the needs of everyday life. Your heavenly Father knows what you have need of. He knows you need to pay the rent or mortgage. He knows you need to shop and buy food that is nourishing and nutritional for your family. He knows you need a car to drive in our society. He knows you need good clothing to wear. Don't be confessing the Word over those things. Seek first His kingdom, and these things will be added to you.

GOD'S HIGHEST WISH FOR YOU

> Beloved, I wish above all things that thou mayest prosper and be in health, even as thy soul prospereth (3 John 2).

Above all things, God wants us to prosper and to be in health. This is our inheritance as children of God, our destiny as His people. How do I know that this verse is for us today? Look at Paul's words to young Timothy:

> All scripture is given by inspiration of God, and is profitable for doctrine, for reproof, for correction, for instruction in righteousness (2 Tim. 3:16).

According to the Apostle John, God's highest wish for you is that you would prosper and be in health. In light of this reality, finances should never stop you from reaching your potential in God. You'll never understand this until you understand the Word of the Lord. If you don't understand the Word of the Lord, you'll never accomplish God's goals. God's highest priority is for you to prosper and to be in health.

AS YOUR SOUL PROSPERS

Look at 3 John 2 again: "EVEN as thy soul prospereth." You cannot prosper and be in health if your soul is not prospering. The word "even," in this context, means equal to how your mind is renewed or is in the process of being renewed. You will prosper and be in health equal to how your soul is prospering.

If you don't know, if you don't understand, if

something has never been revealed to you about what God's purpose, plan and will for your life is, how can you prosper and be in health? Too many of God's people are living below their privileges, beneath their destiny. When you know the Word of God, God can make you equal to His promises.

When Jesus was on this earth, He operated as a man, not as God. The Bible clearly states that He left behind the independent exercise of His divine attributes in order to operate as a man who was anointed with the Holy Ghost: "How God anointed Jesus of Nazareth with the Holy Ghost and with power" (Acts 10:38). Here Luke writes about the humanity of Jesus, not His divinity. Certainly, He is the divine Son of God, the Anointed One, the Messiah. He did not need an anointing, but when He became a man, He was anointed with the Holy Ghost!

As we continue to grow in God, we'll learn that righteousness is the ability to stand in the presence of God without a sense of inferiority, without a sense of guilt and without a sense of condemnation. We'll realize that although we're human beings and have flesh and blood bodies, when Jesus saved us, imparted the Holy Ghost to us, and placed us into God's family, He also put a divine spark of life in us from God the Father. What an exciting, liberating concept this is. No, we're not divine in and of ourselves, but divinity resides within us.

THE BLESSING OF GOOD HEALTH

> . . . If thou wilt diligently hearken to the voice of the LORD thy God, and wilt do that which is right in

his sight, and wilt give ear to his commandments, and keep all his statutes, I will put none of these diseases upon thee, which I have brought upon the Egyptians: for *I am the LORD that healeth thee* (Exod. 15:26, italics mine).

God revealed himself to the Israelites at the waters of Marah as Jehovah-Rapha: "the Lord our healer." Those who believe that this promise was only for the Jews coming out of Egypt would have to call God's name "I WAS" instead of "I AM," which is the name that God gave to Moses at the burning bush (Exod. 3:14).

Then in the Gospel of John, it is recorded that Jesus said to some doubters who were questioning Him, ". . . Verily, verily, I say unto you, Before Abraham was, I am" (John 8:58). This means He is present and perfect. He does not change: "Jesus Christ the same yesterday, and to day, and for ever" (Heb. 13:8). Jesus is now what He always has been and what He always will be. How could God's blessing be dispensational, when in Jesus Christ we have a better covenant—and He who is our Covenant Head is still alive?

On top of that, Psalm 103 tells us not to forget God's benefits, among them the healing of our diseases:

Bless the LORD, O my soul: and all that is within me, bless his holy name. Bless the LORD, O my soul, and forget not all his benefits: Who forgiveth all thine iniquities; *who healeth all thy diseases;* who redeemeth thy life from destruction; who crowneth thee with lovingkindness and tender mercies; who satisfieth thy mouth with good things; so that thy youth is renewed like the eagle's (Ps. 103:1-6, italics mine).

161

Then in Psalms 91:16, God reveals through the Psalmist the result that we should expect from His covenant health plan: "With long life will I satisfy him, and shew him my salvation." Longevity is a part of God's health plan for us—good health and a long life.

The earth's energy levels are being depleted. This has caused more disease within the human race. To the child of God, however, such physical circumstances and scientific discoveries mean little, because the Bible says, "unto you that fear my name shall the Sun of righteousness arise with healing in his wings" (Mal. 4:2). If you will study the original Hebrew, you will discover that light shafts will emanate from His body.

Through Isaiah the prophet, God tells us that His Son wasn't just wounded for our transgressions, He was also "bruised for our iniquities: the chastisement of our peace was upon him; and with his stripes we are healed" (Isa. 53:5). When Peter the apostle quoted from this passage, he wrote, ". . . By whose stripes ye were healed" (1 Pet. 2:24). We have more than just a faith that we will be healed someday, "in the sweet bye and bye," when we get to heaven. We are healed in the present, because the work of Jesus at the whipping post and on Calvary has provided healing for our bodies as well as our souls.

Now there are those in the Church who don't believe in healing today, and many of them say that the passage from Isaiah doesn't refer to physical healing but only to spiritual healing. But look at how Matthew the apostle tied physical healing to Isaiah's words:

> When the even was come, they brought unto him
> many that were possessed with devils: and he cast out

162

the spirits with his word, and healed all that were sick: that it might be fulfilled which was spoken by Esaias (Isaiah) the prophet, saying, Himself took our infirmities, and bare our sicknesses (Matt. 8:16-17).

Jesus' ministry was a ministry of healing. Jesus spent more time talking about healing and finances than any other single subject. The kingdom of God has to have citizens who are healthy and who have enough money to finance the work of the Gospel.

THOU CAN MAKE THY WAY PROSPEROUS

God said to Joshua:

This book of the law shall not depart out of thy mouth; but thou shalt meditate therein day and night, that thou mayest observe to do according to all that is written therein: for then thou shalt make thy way prosperous, and then thou shalt have good success (Josh. 1:8).

In effect, God was saying, "Don't turn to the right and don't turn to the left. Keep this Word in your mouth, and you will make your way prosperous and you will have good success in life."

David told his son Solomon:

And keep the charge of the Lord thy God, to walk in his ways, to keep his statutes, and his commandments, and his judgments, and his testimonies, as it is written in the law of Moses, that thou mayest prosper in all that thou doest, and whithersoever thou turnest thyself: That the Lord may continue his word which he spake concerning me, saying, if thy children take heed to their way, to walk before me in truth with all their heart and with all their soul, there shall not fail thee (said he) a man on the throne of Israel (1 Kings 2:3-4).

God is good. His promises are powerful and He always keeps them. Ezra picks up the positive message of our good God: ". . . The hand of our God is upon all them for good that seek him; but his power and his wrath is against all them that forsake him (Ezra 8:22). The hand of God is upon all them for good that seek Him. For good, not evil.

In Deuteronomy, the Bible message of multiplied blessings continues. (This is a "shouting" verse!):

Therefore thou shalt keep the commandments of the LORD thy God, to walk in his ways, and to fear him. For the LORD thy God bringeth thee into a good land, a land of brooks of water, of fountains and depths that spring out of valleys and hills; A land of wheat, and barley, and vines, and fig trees, and pomegranates; a land of oil olive, and honey; a land wherein thou shalt eat bread without scarceness, thou shalt not lack any thing in it; a land whose stones are iron, and out of whose hills thou mayest dig brass. When thou hast eaten and art full, *then shalt bless the LORD thy God for the good land which he hath given thee* (Deut. 8:6-10, italics mine).

Imagine such a wonderful land! It has honey, pomegranates, vines of figs, olive oil. In that land, if you go out to a hill in your backyard and dig, you strike brass. God said it's "a good land." Has God changed His way of dealing with His people from Old Testament times to now? No. Is the good God of the Old Testament now angry? No. If anything, God in the New Testament is revealed as the Savior of men, the Redeemer! He is a good God. His land flows with milk and honey. There is no scarceness in the kingdom of God. It is the land of more than enough. The Promised Land is ours! But when we come into the land of manifested promises, we are clearly cautioned not to forget something:

> Beware that thou forget not the LORD thy God, in not keeping his commandments, and his judgments, and his statutes, which I command thee this day: Lest when thou hast eaten and art full, and hast built goodly houses, and dwelt therein; And when thy herds and thy flocks multiply, and thy silver and thy gold is multiplied, and all that thou hast is multiplied; Then thine heart be lifted up, and thou forget the Lord thy god, which brought thee forth out of the land of Egypt, from the house of bondage; . . . And thou say in thine heart, My power and the might of mine hand hath gotten me this wealth. But thou shalt remember the Lord thy God: for it is he that giveth thee power to get wealth, that he may establish his covenant which he sware unto thy fathers, as it is this day. (Deut. 8:11-14, 17-18)

Goodly houses for God's people, not shacks. Not just mansions in heaven, but nice homes here. More than enough food—abundant blessings for all. According to your faith, Jesus said, it shall be done unto you. God multiples the blessings; there is no subtraction or division in His kingdom—everything is multiplied! And in Jesus, we are under an even better covenant . This is the will of God for you: multiplied blessings in your life.

But we must never forget that all our multiplied blessings come not from ourselves, but from God—and we must ever be thankful to Him and praise Him for them.

13

Confidence in God

Of all our enemies, perhaps the greatest of is fear, especially fear of other people and what we think they can do to us. It will put us into bondage every time.

> The fear of man bringeth a snare: but whoso putteth his trust in the LORD shall be safe (Prov. 29:25).

> He that dwelleth in the secret place of the most High shall abide under the shadow of the Almighty (Ps. 91:1).

The word "safe" in the Hebrew means "to be set on high." God is the most High, and it's His safety that we seek. The eagle finds a high place, a cleft in a rock, where she keeps her young until they are strong enough to be out on their own. In the cleft of the rock, they are protected from the dangers and storms of life. Similarly, when you have trust and confidence in God—that is, have faith in Him—He brings you to a high place.

No More Fear or Inferiority

Fear of other people stems from an inferiority complex, and keeps many Christians from reaching their ultimate goal and destiny in God because they believe they are incapable of doing something profitable to help someone else. Having an inferiority complex means you have a failure image. You can't see yourself being a success. This is primarily motivated by something on the inside of you that says, "Everyone is better than me." This is what the Scripture calls "the fear of man."

God has provided us with abundant ways to lift ourselves out of timidity, shame, and low self-esteem. In this chapter, we are going to look at these ways through the lens of the Word of God.

Walking Out From Under Your Protection

In Judges 6, we learn about a man who had a situation in his life that could have really broken him. The man is Gideon. He and the children of Israel were in a horrible plight.

> And the children of Israel did evil in the sight of the LORD: and the LORD delivered them into the hand of Midian seven years (Judg. 6:1).

Walking away from God's grace is usually a gradual process. The day you first walk out from His grace, nothing may happen you. You may look the same and other people may look at you and say, "Why didn't God deal with him?"

But no one gets away with anything with God—he reaps the negative he sows unless he repents and gets his heart right. The Scriptures tell us that everything that is hidden will be revealed (Matt. 10:26, Luke 12:2) It may not happen right away, God may let you go your own way for awhile—but the reaping is ahead of you somewhere.

It's like having to make a payment on a bill and you don't have the money when the payment is due. A grace period now goes into effect. During that period, you can still pay without incurring a late payment penalty. However, if you go past the last day of the grace period, you'll have to pay the penalty.

In a similar way, God offers His grace over a length of time. It may not be seven days or thirty days—only God knows the length. Ultimately, however, He will come for His check, and then it's either get your heart right with God immediately, or pay the penalty.

The Bible is a sequential record of how God dealt with His people in the past and, thus, how God deals with His people now. Look at the promises of God and the covenant He made with Israel. He, in effect, told them, "All you have to do is follow me, observe My commandments and I will bless and protect you." But, time and again, His people sinned against Him and ended up in captivity to another nation.

That's what happened in the story of Gideon. The Lord had delivered the Israelites into the hands of Midian for seven years.

And the hand of Midian prevailed against Israel:
and because of the Midianites the children of Israel

made them the dens which are in the mountains, and caves, and strong holds. And so it was, when Israel had sown, that the Midianites came up, and the Amalekites, and the children of the east, even they came up against them; And they encamped against them, and destroyed the increase of the earth, till thou come unto Gaza, and left no sustenance for Israel, neither sheep, nor ox, nor ass (Judg. 6:2-4).

Every time they went out into the fields and planted wheat or other seed and it began to produce, the Amalekites and Midianites came and destroyed their crops and tore up their fields.

We don't like to talk about God causing something like this to happen. "Well, that wasn't God, it was the devil," we rationalize. The Scriptures clearly show, however, that it was God lifting His protection from His people. The Amalekites and Midianites could not have come in if God's angels were protecting the Israelites. God had told His people to drive His enemies out of the Promised Land. The moment Israel forgot God, however, God's protection stopped because He had told His people that would result if they forgot Him and turned to other gods. And God always keeps His Word.

God's Reminders

For they came up with their cattle and their tents, and they came as grasshoppers for multitude; for both they and their camels were without number: and they entered into the land to destroy it. And Israel was greatly impoverished because of the Midianites; and the children of Israel cried unto the LORD (Judg. 6:5-6).

170

This is what I call "crisis faith." Do I only want God when I need Him, or do I want Him because I love Him? They cried to the Lord; you and I would have cried to the Lord, too. They had nothing to eat. Their animals were dying. The Amalekites and Midianites were so great in number they were like grasshoppers coming across the land. There were so many camels they could not be counted. The children of Israel knew that they were in big trouble and they cried unto the Lord.

By so doing, they put a key to answered prayer into operation. No matter how far away from God you go, or how far down you get, or how bad you have been, all you need to do is cry out to God and He'll incline His ear toward you. Don't tell me you've gone too far from God. Don't tell me that God doesn't love you. Don't tell me you've been too bad. Don't tell me there's no hope for you. God is a God of mercy and grace. Do what the Israelites did, turn back to God and cry out to Him:

> And it came to pass, when the children of Israel cried unto the LORD because of the Midianites, that the LORD sent a prophet unto the children of Israel, which said unto them, Thus saith the LORD God of Israel, I brought you up from Egypt, and brought you forth out of the house of bondage (Judg. 6:7-8).

Throughout the Old Testament, God constantly reminds His people of all He did for them. God has blessed us with good memories to enable us always to remember what He has done for us. There's an old song that says, "When I remember what He's done for me, I'll never turn back anymore." That's an important

171

principle: we need always to remember from where God has brought us.

Some of us become haughty and proud once in awhile. God saved us when we were nothing and brought us out of misery and despair. Then we get into a church, get all cleaned up, get a good job, and soon become the judge and jury for everybody else. We have no tolerance for anybody anymore. Someone misses God, we jump on the bandwagon of condemnation. We want to separate them from fellowship, and sometimes even kick them out of our church. If that's our superior attitude, we need to look in the mirror of God's Word and see the dirt on our own face and the plank in our own eye.

God continued to remind His people what He had done for them:

> And I delivered you out of the hand of the Egyptians, and out of the hand of all that oppressed you, and drave them out from before you, and gave you their land; And I said unto you, I am the LORD your God; fear not the gods of the Amorites, in whose land ye dwell: but ye have not obeyed my voice (Judg. 6:9-10).

He will not let you forget. Even when you try to forget, He will not let you do so. When you cry out to Him, the first thing He may do is bring to your mind all the things that He has done for you in the past, and perhaps remind you of the many times you doubted Him and turned away from Him—and even talked against Him by blaming Him for something.

No wonder Jeremiah said, "It is of the LORD's mercies that we are not all consumed, because his compassions fail not" (Lam. 3:22). We can't understand the patience of God. Think about His patience with you for a moment. When I consider His patience in my life, I think of all the times I've missed God and He's been patient with me.

God is loving, patient, kind and just. But be careful about praying that God bring justice against someone. One time, several years ago, someone deeply hurt me. I wanted to hurt them in return so much that it temporarily blinded me to God's ways. I had a legalistic cliché left over somewhere back in the reservoir of my religious thinking, and I said to God, "Lord, I pray, in the name of Jesus, that you will enforce justice in their life."

I no sooner got the words out of my mouth when the Spirit of the Lord rose up on the inside of me and said, "If I enforce justice on him, I have to enforce justice on Dave Demola."

I *immediately* changed my prayer, "Lord, enforce your grace. I thank you for your grace."

That was a moment of revelation for me. It was a rhema word to my spirit. If God has to act by justice, that means He has to treat everyone the same way. That would mean we'll be accountable for everything we've ever done. Justice means punishment for the guilty, and we're all guilty. The Bible says, "For all have sinned, and come short of the glory of God" (Rom. 3:23). But, for us, That's where Jesus walks in and says, "Father, I'll like to speak on that person's behalf."

Now let's look at how God delivered Israel from the Midianites:

> And there came an angel of the LORD, and sat under an oak which was in Ophrah, that pertained unto

> Joash the Abiezrite: and his son Gideon threshed
> wheat by the winepress, to hide it from the Midianites
> (Judg. 6:11).

I used to think Gideon was a coward, but when you look this story over closely, you find out what the Midianites and the Amalekites were doing. If you looked out of your window one night and saw a herd of camels coming at you that you could not even number, and an army of men that looked like grasshoppers across the field, you also would have been hiding while you threshed wheat.

WE SEE OURSELVES AS WE ARE—GOD SEES US AS HE MADE US

Gideon was hiding while he threshed wheat because every time the Midianites and Amorites came they stole all the wheat they could find. So Gideon was reaping the wheat the second it was ripe enough and threshing it in hiding. He was smarter and braver than some of us would have been—we would have just been hiding. In the midst of his threshing, God sent an angel to him. We can hide from human beings but we can't hide from God. "And the angel of the LORD appeared unto him, and said unto him, The LORD is with thee, *thou mighty man of valour*" (Judg. 6:12, italics mine).

Mighty man of valor? Gideon was hiding. We forget that God sees in you and me what other humans and even we ourselves can't see. What a divine announcement to Gideon: "The Lord is with thee, thou mighty man of valour."

> And Gideon said unto him, Oh my Lord, if the
> LORD be with us, why then is all this befallen us?
> (Judg. 6:13).

Gideon questioned a bit what the angel proclaimed, and immediately wanted some answers. He wanted to know why all this opposition was taking place if God was with them. And besides that, "...where be all his miracles which our fathers told us of, saying, Did not the LORD bring us up from Egypt . . . ?" (Judg. 6:13).

The Israelites had been in Midian for seven years. Gideon is obviously a young man. All he has known throughout his life is misery, strife, poverty, stolen crops and destroyed animals, and a father who worshipped Baal (Judg. 6:25). Everything Gideon has ever known has been negative. In such a time of pressure, out of the negative abundance of the heart, the mouth voices doubts and questions, as did Gideon's: ". . . But now the LORD hath forsaken us, and delivered us into the hands of the Midianites" (Judg. 6:13).

The LORD doesn't respond to Gideon's complains, doubts, or questions. The Scripture says, "And the LORD looked upon him, and said, Go in this thy might . . ." (Judg. 6:14). The LORD's refusal to move down to Gideon's level is a good point for us to remember when we're complaining, doubting, and questioning.

By not answering, the LORD, in effect, was telling Gideon something that he did not know about himself, something that God had made him but that had never manifested within him, "You are a mighty man of valor—not a weak moaner, bellyacher or complainer."

And the *Lord* looked upon him, and said, Go in
this thy might, and *thou* (*thou,* not your people, not
your family, not your nation, but *thou*), shalt save
Israel from the hand of the Midianites: have not I sent
thee? (Judg. 6:14, italics mine).

Picture this. Gideon is hearing the angel in his left
ear and watching him out of his left eye. With his other
ear and eye, he hears and sees numberless Amalekites,
Midianites and camels. Besides that, he doesn't have
anything to fight with, and nobody thinks much of him,
so naturally he tells the LORD these things as if the
LORD doesn't already know them: "And he said unto
him, Oh my Lord, wherewith shall I save Israel? behold,
my family is poor in Manasseh, and I am the least in
my father's house" (Judg. 6:15).

Gideon had low self-esteem. He did not have a
negative self-image because he woke up one day and
decided to have it. Like the rest of us, he was a product
of his environment. Our children will suffer from the
things we, as parents, do and do not do. But still, Gideon
did not have to be poor in any way—emotionally,
spiritually or financially.

THE COVENANT

When God gave Abraham "The Covenant" in
Genesis 12, that covenant went down to every family in
the lineage of Israel. Gideon had a right to grow up in a
house where there was abundance. Gideon was poor
because his father and all the Israelites had forsaken God.
They had turned their backs on God's covenant. The
result is that Gideon himself was in a very difficult place.

176

No one wants to fail in life. We all want to succeed at whatever we do. We want our children to grow up and become the best they can. These are natural desires. None of us wants to be a failure in life.

Many of us, however, are like Gideon. The products of an environment that makes us feel like failures. Even if an angel talks to you as to Gideon, you still can't see yourself as being victorious, let alone as being a mighty man or woman of valor.

The Bible has an encouraging word for anyone who suffers from an inferiority complex, which is nothing but lack of confidence in our own internal strength: "I can do all things through Christ which (who) strengtheneth me" (Phil. 4:13). Look at what the LORD told Gideon, who never knew what God had already made him: ". . . *surely,* I will be with thee, and thou shalt smite the Midianites as one man" (Judg. 6:16, italics mine). When we are sure and certain that God is with us, we can do anything.

The LORD told Gideon that he would smite the entire army of the Midianites as if they were only "one man." When God empowers us, anything confronting us—an army of enemies, an overwhelming situation, seemingly impossible odds—regardless of size or form, gets cut down to size. We are then able to handle the situation in the strength of the Lord.

DON'T SAY YOU AREN'T AND YOU CAN'T—WHEN GOD SAYS YOU ARE AND YOU CAN

Gideon tried to insist that He wasn't what the Lord said He was, but the Lord wouldn't listen. He tried to insist that He could not do what the LORD said he could do, and the LORD wouldn't listen. The LORD knew that regardless of what Gideon thought and felt about himself, he was what God had made him and could do what God would enable him to do.

When God says you're blessed, fifty-million people in the world and fifty-million fallen angels cannot reverse it. If God says you're blessed, He'll bless you.

We need to change our thinking. We need to tell ourselves: "Wherever I go, blessings follow me." When you walk into someone's house to visit them, say, "The blessing of the Lord be on this house." You need to bless the house. You need to bless someone's car, bless someone's children. "The blessing of the Lord be on this house. The peace of the Lord is in this house." Make positive statements of faith.

That's how we walk out of fear. We need to walk away from the fear that we'll never make it. If God is for us, who can be against us?

The same Almighty LORD who chose Gideon to defeat the Midianite army, chose you to go forth into life and bear much fruit. Your fruit will remain. He has chosen you to be his friend. He has already given you victories that you haven't even walked in. Our job is to walk in all the victories and blessings which He has bestowed upon us.

I love the story about what happened to Peter when he went up on the rooftop to pray:

> He became hungry and wanted something to eat, and while the meal was being prepared, he fell into a trance. He saw heaven opened and something like a

large sheet being let down to earth by its four corners. It contained all kinds of four-footed animals, as well as reptiles of the earth and birds of the air. Then a voice told him, "Get up, Peter. Kill and eat." "Surely not, Lord!" Peter replied. "I have never eaten anything impure or unclean." The voice spoke to him a second time, "Do not call anything impure that God has made clean" (Acts 10:10-15, NIV).

That statement applies to us as well. God values us. He created us. His Son died for us. As a result, God cleansed us and made us righteous and translated us into the kingdom of His beloved Son. He gave us worth and meaning. These facts will lift your sense of self-esteem. It doesn't make any difference what I decide about you or what you decide about me—or what other people decide about either of us. The only thing that should matter to you and me is what God thinks about us.

Some of us have cut short what God wanted to do in our lives because a lack of self-confidence and a feeling of inadequacy have held us back. God has been waiting for you to release yourself. Don't hold back any more. Don't wait any longer for God to manifest in you and in your life what He has already decreed for you.

You may think, "I'd like to do something for God, but I don't have the confidence I need. You need to tell yourself something else, "I can and I will do all things through Christ who strengthens me." That is how you need to talk to yourself in order to see yourself as God sees you. God does not see your failures and your faults. He sees your potential—the potential that He has put in you.

GET OUT OF GOD'S WAY

There is only one thing that can stop you from moving from where you are to where God wants you to be, and that's you.

Remove every obstacle.

Remove every doubt.

Remove yourself out of God's way.

Say to yourself right now, "From now on, I will not allow any human—including myself—or devil to stand between me and my ultimate victory in God." Resolve this matter in your heart right now. God will take care of the rest. He'll move heaven and earth on behalf of His children if they call out to Him in faith. He'll accomplish His purposes for your life

You can fulfill your destiny in God if you will place your total trust and confidence in Him.

Every promise He has uttered is for you.

Abandon yourself to Him.

14

God Equips
Those He Calls

God's School of Preparation

Moses was chosen and ordained by God to deliver Israel from Egypt. But first, God must instill leadership qualities into his life through a process of training and learning. When we read the Bible, we sometimes forget the circumstances that transpired before victorious events occurred. How did God lead people to become useful tools in His hand? We tend to look at their successes without examining the steps that got them there. We look at the end results, but we may fail to see how the leaders were developed. Moses, like all leaders, had to develop the qualities that were required for the challenges he faced.

It's important for us to understand this truth. Otherwise, we miss a vital part of how God prepares us for all that we are to become and do in Him. This is what I call God's "School of Preparation." You are enrolled in a school that has produced countless leaders who have accomplished great things for God—Abraham, Moses, Joshua, David, Gideon, Paul, Peter, just to name a few.

THE DELIVERER

"Now Moses kept the flock of Jethro his father-in-law" (Exod. 3:1). A sheepherder who works for his father-in-law doesn't seem like a mighty deliverer. And Moses probably didn't feel like one either. He may have even asked himself, "What am I doing here? I know what God has called me to do, so why am I where I am now?" There have been several occasions in my life when I knew that I was supposed to be achieving certain goals, and yet I found myself in a place much like Moses'.

You probably know what that's like. You may ask, "What am I doing here? What in the world is God doing with me?" At such a time you wonder how long, when, why and how come.

> Now Moses kept the flock of Jethro his father in law, the priest of Midian: and he led the flock to the backside of the desert, and came to the mountain of God, even to Horeb (Exod. 3:1).

It's bad enough to be tending sheep for one's father-in-law, but to have to do so on "the backside of the desert" must have been very disheartening and lonely. But as in all of God's journeys, there was a purpose for each step. And therein is a tremendous lesson for all of us. When, in one or several areas of your life, there seems to be nowhere to turn or go, and you seem to be stuck in the backside of the most barren and unproductive desert imaginable, it may be that God has brought you there to "His mountain" to do something great in your life. This was certainly the case with Moses.

> And the angel of the LORD appeared unto him in a flame of fire out of the midst of a bush: and he looked, and, behold, the bush burned with fire, and the bush was not consumed (Exod. 3:2).

On one of the probably long days of Moses' shepherding, he was suddenly surprised by a supernatural manifestation of God. If you're in a similar place, God may be getting ready to speak to you, to tell you His plan for you, to disclose His purpose for your life.

THE HOLINESS OF GOD

> And Moses said, I will now turn aside, and see this great sight, why the bush is not burnt. And when the Lord saw that he turned aside to see, God called unto him out of the midst of the bush, and said, Moses, Moses. And he said, here am I. And he said, Draw not nigh hither: put off thy shoes from off thy feet, for the place whereon thou standest is holy ground (Exod. 3:3-5).

Moses came face to face with the holiness of God. We sometimes get too chummy with God. We fail to see His majesty and splendor. God is not our "buddy." We must not treat Him like some human or even supernatural pal. God was showing Moses that there's a line of separation between the profane and the holy. The unclean must be separated from the clean.

God wants us to know Him as our heavenly Father, the One who is to be worshiped, honored, adored, praised and glorified in His position of honor. Though He is not a "buddy," He is our Friend, and we can talk to Him and confide in Him. But there are principles that we must observe in this relationship .

If you want to get anything from God and you want to get to know God properly, you're going to have to meet Him on the grounds of His holiness. When we try to approach God on a buddy-to-buddy basis as happens all too often today, we lose sight of so many important things, such as the holiness of God and the appropriate response to Him.

> Moreover he said, I am the God of thy father, the God of Abraham, the God of Isaac, and the God of Jacob. And Moses hid his face; for he was afraid to look upon God (Exod. 3:6).

When Moses heard that it was God speaking, He hid his face in fear; Saul of Tarsus fell to the earth when the bright light of Jesus shone around him on the Damascus Road; and the Apostle John fell as one dead before the glorified Christ on the Isle of Patmos. When you truly come face to face with God, you're not cocky and arrogant. You feel insignificant and often fearful in His glorious presence.

Moses was afraid to look upon God because He was God—the holy and Almighty God of Abraham, Isaac, and Jacob. The Church today needs a relationship with God that is like that . Too many of us only want to know God for what we can get from Him—a God whom we can petition and who will give us gifts. We've forgotten that first and foremost we are to know Him as the high and holy God that Isaiah and all the prophets wrote about and walked before in awe and fear—the God they did not dare to disobey.

This was Moses' approach to God. Notice how God responded:

> And the LORD said, I have surely seen the affliction of my people which are in Egypt, and have heard their cry by reason of their taskmasters; for I know their sorrows; And I am come down to deliver them out of the hand of the Egyptians, and to bring them up out of that land unto a good land and a large, unto a land flowing with milk and honey; unto the place of the Canaanites, and the Hittites, and the Amorites, and the Perizzites, and the Hivites, and the Jebusites. Now therefore, behold, the cry of the children of Israel is come unto me: and I have also seen the oppression wherewith the Egyptians oppress them. Come now therefore, and I will send thee unto Pharaoh, that thou mayest bring forth my people the children of Israel out of Egypt (Exod. 3:7-10).

The first thing that God stressed was the fact that the Israelites were His people, not Moses' people. That's an important distinction. I try to train young ministers to stop going around saying, "My ministry, my congregation, my church." These God-given fields don't belong to a person. We were saved by the blood of Jesus, and we're in the family of God. We belong to Him alone.

Every word that God spoke to Moses in the above passage has a powerful meaning and message for us today. Do you know why God spoke to Moses the things that He did? Because these were the things that Moses had been concerned about, and God knew his heart. Moses had been talking to God about each of these matters, and God always responds to our cries: "God, what are you going to do about my people and the oppression? What are you going to do about all the things that are going on with all of my brothers and sisters? When are you going to answer my prayer? God, when are you going to deliver them out of the bondage of Egypt?"

God so much as told Moses, "You've been worrying and asking me when and how I'm going to deliver these people. I want you to know, I've heard their cry. I've seen their affliction. I'll come down and deliver them. I'll send you to Pharaoh and you'll deliver them by my hand."

Let's keep this wonderful passage in mind when we're in the midst of a problem and we don't know where to turn. When we don't know what to do, how to get out and what the answer is, God will come on the scene. He'll announce His plans and tell us what's in His heart. God will come through.

TIME IS IN GOD'S HANDS

If you're in the midst of tough times right now and you don't know how to get out, and you've called on the Lord and it seems like the heavens are silent, always remember that God is not sleeping. Time is in God's hands, and His timing is perfect.

There may be a period of seeming silence, where you might not see something happen when you want it to happen, but when God finally comes on the scene and

186

He reveals His purpose and plan to you, it'll be in such clear terms that no one will have to try to figure it out.

God assured Moses that he would deliver His people, but He also told Moses that He was going to use him to do it. Notice how Moses' reply to God fits in with the theme verse of the previous chapter: "The fear of man [Or an inferiority complex, or timidity] bringeth a snare: but whoso putteth his trust in the LORD shall be safe" (Prov. 29:25).

> And Moses said unto God, Who am I, that I should go unto Pharaoh, and that I should bring forth the children of Israel out of Egypt? (Exod. 3:11).

FEAR OF QUALIFICATIONS

Moses' leading protest was that he wasn't qualified: "Who am I that I should go unto Pharaoh, and that I should bring forth the children of Israel out of Egypt?" Since Moses spoke of Pharaoh, who had tried to kill him forty years before, He may also have been afraid that God meant that he had to convince Pharaoh to let all the Israelite slaves leave Egypt. But that wasn't what God meant, all that Moses had to do was lead the people out after God set them free. But, regardless, Moses wasn't too happy about his assignment and needed a bit of convincing from God.

> And he said, Certainly I will be with thee; and this shall be a token unto thee, that I have sent thee: When thou hast brought forth the people out of Egypt, ye shall serve God upon this mountain. And Moses said

187

unto God, Behold, when I come unto the children of Israel, and shall say unto them, The God of your fathers hath sent me unto you; and they shall say to me, What is his name? What shall I say unto them? (Exod. 3:12-13).

Moses had a short memory, just like most of us. God had just told him who He was: "I am the God of Abraham, the God of Isaac and the God of Jacob." Moses was hedging, still trying to find reasons why God shouldn't send Him. God wouldn't listen when he complained about his lack of qualifications, so now he picked on the issue of God's name; that is, what name he should give the Israelites if they should ask him, "What is the name of the God of our fathers?"

In other words, "When they ask me for my qualifications and credentials, when they ask me which organization sent me or what my denominational background is, who shall I say sent me?" "And God said unto Moses, I AM THAT I AM: and he said, Thus shalt thou say unto the children of Israel, I AM hath sent me unto you (Exod. 3:14).

You have to listen to God's response to identify what God was saying to Moses. God does not usually speak in long sentences and paragraphs. He usually speaks in a few choice lines, and those few lines have to be carefully examined to find out what He really means.

Ancient Egyptian culture believed that when a Pharaoh died, and a young Pharaoh replaced him, the young Pharaoh was a reincarnation of the old Pharaoh. Because of this belief in royal reincarnation, they would often use the expression "I am" to refer to the Pharaoh. The present tense indicated a perpetual, never-ending royal lineage for the throne.

Undoubtedly, Moses had this concept in the back of his head. He may not have believed it, but it may well have been a part of his thinking. This concept restricted him from allowing faith to operate in what God was saying to him.

When Moses asked, "Who shall I tell them sent me?"

God answered: "I AM THAT I AM." He was, in effect, telling Moses, "You tell them I am THAT I am."

The Egyptians believed Pharaoh was the *I am.* God was saying, in effect, "I am THAT I am." By using the demonstrative pronoun, God was being specific. He was saying, "I am not the I am that Pharaoh says he is. I am identifying myself as the only I am. I am THAT I am."

By making this distinction for Moses, God was telling Moses not to be intimidated or afraid of his qualifications and credentials. When he stands up before the Israelites, get all of Egypt out of him. Get rid of that stinking thinking and that wrong way of seeing things.

GETTING EGYPT OUT OF YOU

God so much as told Moses, "You will not have to worry about your qualifications. They are not even going to look to you. You are incapable of doing anything on your own. You just tell them I AM the real I AM."

When God sends you, you don't have to apologize to anyone. God is behind you, before you, beside you, within you and watching over you.

> And God said moreover unto Moses, Thus shalt thou say unto the children of Israel, The LORD God of your fathers, the God of Abraham, the God of Isaac,

and the God of Jacob, hath sent me unto you: this is my name for ever, and this is my memorial unto all generations. Go, and gather the elders of Israel together, and say unto them, The LORD God of your fathers, the God of Abraham, of Isaac and of Jacob, appeared unto me, saying, I have surely visited you, and seen that which is done to you in Egypt: and I have said, I will bring you up out of the affliction of Egypt unto the land of the Canaanites, and the Hittites, and the Amorites, and the Perizzites, and the Hivites, and the Jebusites, unto a land flowing with milk and honey. And they shall hearken to thy voice: and thou shalt come, thou and the elders of Israel, unto the king of Egypt, and ye shall say unto him, *The LORD God of the Hebrews hath met with us* . . . (Exod. 3:15-18, italics mine).

When is the Body of Christ going to stop being ashamed or afraid to declare what God has said, in spite of what people will think? Are we afraid of being considered crazy? Once you get saved, many people think you're nuts; so you may as well go all the way with God.

Moses was to tell the Egyptians, "The God of the Hebrews met with us." God wanted to identify himself as being different from the false gods of the Egyptians. He did not want to be mixed with their false gods. Then He explained his deliverance plan:

And I will stretch out my hand, and smite Egypt with all my wonders which I will do in the midst thereof: and after that he will let you go. And I will give this people favour in the sight of the Egyptians: and it shall come to pass, that, when ye go, ye shall not go empty: But every woman shall borrow of her neighbour, and of her that sojourneth in her house, jewels of silver, and jewels of gold, and raiment: and ye shall put them upon your sons, and upon your daughters; and ye shall spoil the Egyptians (Exod. 3:20-22).

God wasn't telling them to steal these things. He was telling them to borrow them. Amazingly, when they did borrow these items, the Egyptians must have said something like, "We don't want it back. Keep it. Take it all with you. Just get out of here."

FEAR OF FAILURE

After all he had heard and seen, Moses still needed more assurance from God. Fear was still holding him back. At first his fear was based on what he perceived to be his lack of qualifications, but when God dealt with that, he had to face what may have been his real fear: fear of failure. "And Moses answered and said, But, behold, they will not believe me, nor hearken unto my voice: for they will say, The LORD hath not appeared unto thee" (Exod. 4:1). Moses hadn't yet graduated from God's "School of Preparation."

Moses complained that the Israelites wouldn't believe that the LORD had appeared to him, therefore God had to reassure him by giving him something by which he could prove to the Israelites that the LORD had appeared to him and sent him to them—so God said, "what is that in thine hand? And he said, A rod" (Exod. 4:2). Notice that God didn't ask him for something he didn't have. God will use what you have.

> And he said, Cast it on the ground. And he cast it
> on the ground, and it became a serpent; and Moses
> fled from before it. And the Lord said unto Moses, put
> forth thine hand, and take it by the tail. And he put
> forth his hand, and caught it, and it became a rod in
> his hand: That they may believe that the LORD God
> of their fathers, the God of Abraham, the God of Isaac,
> and the God of Jacob, hath appeared unto thee (Exod.
> 4:3-5).

God doesn't perform miracles just to do miracles. There's always a purpose behind His supernatural power being revealed—it's always a sign of something (John 20:30-31).

God can take something that is common and make it supernatural in your hands. When God gets into something, He can take what's normal, natural and common, and make it supernatural, divine and holy. Moses' rod became a miracle rod. From this point on, it was no longer the rod of Moses, it was now "the rod of God" (Exod. 4:20). When God gives you a gift, He never identifies it as being yours or belonging to you. He always identifies it as His gift that is given to be used by you.

FEAR OF REJECTION

> And it shall come to pass, if they will not believe
> also these two signs, neither hearken unto thy voice,
> that thou shalt take of the water of the river, and pour
> it upon the dry land: and the water which thou takest
> out of the river shall become blood upon the dry land.
> And Moses said unto the LORD, O my Lord, I am
> not eloquent, neither heretofore, nor since thou hast

spoken unto thy servant: but I am slow of speech, and of a slow tongue (Exod. 4:9-10).

Many us never get ahead in God because we keep our eyes on our perceived weaknesses instead of His strength. God keeps telling us that He is going to do it, and we keep saying, "I can't. I don't know how. I don't know what to do."

God can make a donkey talk to a prophet. He can cause a fish to open its mouth and produce gold coins to pay taxes. He can have ravens feed a prophet. He can call a whole school of fish to go alongside a boat and fill up a net. He can send manna, a pillar of fire, water from a rock. He can part the Red Sea.

Why, then, do we think we need a Ph.D. to speak for Him. I don't need formal schooling to be used by Him—He has a special "School of Preparation." What I must have is a heart that is open, willing and obedient to God. That's what God was looking for in Moses, and He wants us to have the same heart-attitude.

If we ever expect to move ahead in God, if the end-time revival that is about to hit us is to come in with a force that we have never seen before, it's going to have to be accomplished through men and women who are blessed in every area of life.

The Church will never pay all its bills and do everything God has said it's going to do until God blesses men and women both financially and spiritually in the pursuits of life. Wherever you are today, set your vision and your goal high. See the hand of God on you. Don't worry about your lack of qualifications, other people or the things you feel you lack.

Rely on the God who has told us in many ways: "I'm going to do it. I'll bring you out. I'll raise you up. I'll set My hand upon you. No man shall be able to stand against you. I'll put My word, the Sword of the Spirit, in your mouth. I'll put the shield of faith on your arm. I'll give you everything you need, and you'll be able to combat every foe that rises against you and you'll come out on top."

God equips those He calls—

He'll call you.

He'll get you ready in His "School of Preparation."

He'll give you the gifts you need to do the work.

He'll send you where He wants you to go.

And He'll go with you to do all that He promised you He would do.

15

Raising the Lord's Standard

> So shall they fear the name of the LORD from the
> west, and his glory from the rising of the sun. When
> the enemy shall come in like a flood, the Spirit of the
> LORD shall lift up a standard against him (Isa. 59:19).

There *are* times when the enemy comes in like a
flood. But we must never focus on a flood, even when
we know it's coming. Doing so will too often intimidate,
scare, and worry most of us—or, at the least, cause us a
great deal of concern and even anxiety.

Forget about any flood that may be headed your way.
If you examine the Scripture closely, you'll see that it
says that the Spirit of the Lord will raise up a standard
against the flood. God has a remedy. He has a standard
that will defeat the enemy—an antidote against his
poison.

In His sermon on the mount, Jesus said,

> Therefore whosoever heareth these sayings of
> mine, and doeth them, I will liken him unto a wise

man, which built his house upon a rock: And the rain descended, and the floods came, and the winds blew, and beat upon that house; and it fell not: for it was founded upon a rock (Matt. 7:24-25).

Jesus did not say, *"If* the rain descends." He did not say, *"If* the wind blows." He did not say, *"If* the flood comes." He clearly said, "And the rain descended, and the floods came, and the winds blew." There is no question about the fact that rain, wind and floods are coming. He did not say there was a *possibility* of them coming—He said *they came.*

"Therefore whosoever heareth . . ." (Matt. 7:24). That word "heareth" doesn't mean to identify sounds by the human ear. It means to understand and act upon what you hear. Many Christians only listen to those things they like to hear, and do only those things that make them feel good.

There's another word in this passage that's important to understand—it's the word "wise," which means prudent and sensible Christians are supposed to be sensible about practical matters—they're supposed to have common sense. It's amazing to see how many people are having financial trouble because they're not practical. Then they blame the devil for their woes. When you make $500 a week and you spend $600, don't say the devil is stealing from you. It's not the devil; you're just not using common sense. You're not being practical.

Wise people are not only people who have intelligence, they are practical. They are prudent. They are sensible. They have common sense. When you talk to wise people

196

about the ways of God or practical matters in Christianity, they listen.

Notice the contrast Jesus develops here: "And every one that heareth these sayings of mine, and doeth them not, shall be likened unto a foolish man, which built his house upon the sand" (Matt. 7:26).

Some people start out building their house on the Rock, but they end up on the sand. How does this happen? They hear the Word of God, and in the beginning when things are easy they do what it says; but later when things get a bit tougher, they go the easy way of their own hearts and the world's philosophy. They follow the advice of friends. Soon they are "blown about by every wind of doctrine" (Eph. 4:14), and never find stability in God.

Jesus said that such a person,

> ... shall be likened unto a foolish man, which built his house upon the sand: And the rain descended, and the floods came, and the winds blew, and beat upon that house; and it fell: and great was the fall of it (Matt. 7:26-27).

Where do you find yourself today? How stable is your spiritual house? If it shakes every time a mild storm comes along, then you'd better look closely at what it is built upon. Each of us can determine what type of ground our spiritual house is built upon by what happens to it during the daily rains and winds. If it's built on sand, then we had better get it over onto the rock because hurricane-force storms are coming.

The Mississippi River floods of 1993 showed us how

devastating floods can be. Many people lost not only their houses, but everything they had spent a lifetime accumulating. All truths are parallel: the same thing can happen with spiritual houses. There are all types of spiritual floods. God wants us to be ready for them. Wind, rain and rising water are potentially disastrous. A house which is built on the Rock, even when assaulted by all three elements, cannot be moved off the Rock. Are you on the Rock today, or are you on shifting sand?

THE BREATH OF ALMIGHTY GOD

In Isa. 59:19 it is written, ". . . The Spirit of the LORD shall lift up a standard against him." A modern translation shows that this means that the breath of the Almighty will go out against the enemy. That breath is the Holy Spirit.

God's breath is the wind that stirred the mulberry trees (2 Sam. 5:24). It was the breath of God, the *pneuma*, that the people heard on the Day of Pentecost as the Holy Spirit descended from heaven.

There is an interesting passage in the 32nd chapter of the Book of Job that has to do with the relationship between the Holy Spirit—the breath of God—and His effect upon our spirit.

> And Elihu the son of Barachel the Buzite answered and said, I am young, and ye are very old; wherefore I was afraid, and durst not shew you mine opinion. I said, Days should speak, and multitude of years should teach wisdom. But there is a spirit in man: and the inspiration of the Almighty giveth them understanding (Job 32:6-8).

198

You're not just a body; there's a spirit in you. The spirit within is what gives you spiritual understanding. This kind of understanding means a practical knowledge— being able to perceive something and determine what to do. It's the kind of spiritual understanding that Jesus referred to when He said, "Suppose one of you wants to build a tower. Will he not first sit down and estimate the cost to see if he has enough money to complete it?" (Luke 14:28, NIV).

The spirit of man, when joined with the Spirit of God, accomplishes great things. But as Elihu said, "Great men are not always wise . . ." (Job 32:9). People in high places are not always smart. Without spiritual understanding, there's no true wisdom.

My Uncle Jimmy is going to be eighty soon. He never finished school, but in his lifetime, he has probably made more money than most. He's a practical man. He's always encouraging me in the Lord. Some great men, however, are not always wise.

The Scriptures tell us that just because you have a high position, or because you're an older person, doesn't of itself mean that you're wise or have understanding of spiritual matters.

> Great men are not always wise: neither do the aged understand judgment . . . I said, I will answer also my part, I also will shew mine opinion. For I am full of matter, the spirit within me constraineth me (Job 32:9, 17-18).

"The spirit within me constraineth me." Constrain, in this context, does not mean to keep one back. In the Hebrew, it means that Elihu was so filled with words that he was compelled to speak them. There is a spirit in man, and this spirit gives us understanding. It fills us so much with words that those words must come out.

Exodus 14 helps us to see how this works. The children of Israel had left Egypt and were on their way to the Promised Land. The Lord lead them to the edge of the Red Sea—a strange place for Him to take them. But when you leave your life in God's hands, you never have to worry about what He does with you or where He leads you. *When God guides, He provides.* The Israelites, like all of us, had to learn this important lesson.

Millions of Israelites were on this journey. All of a sudden they began to realize that the Red Sea was in front of them. Just as bad, there were mountains on both sides of them, and—even worse—when they looked back the way they came they saw the chariots of Pharaoh headed their way. A mountain on the left, a mountain on the right, the Red Sea straight ahead, and Pharaoh and his army behind them in rapid pursuit. Things looked a bit desperate—but God was about to teach them a lesson of always looking to Him for protection and the way out of every situation.

> And the LORD hardened the heart of Pharaoh king of Egypt, and he pursued after the children of Israel: and the children of Israel went out with an high hand. But the Egyptians pursued after them, all the horses and chariots of Pharaoh, and his horsemen, and his army, and overtook them encamping by the sea, beside Pi-hahiroth, before Baal-zephon. And when Pharaoh drew nigh, the children of Israel lifted up their eyes, and, behold, the Egyptians marched after them; and they were sore afraid: and the children of Israel cried

out unto the LORD. And they said unto Moses, Because there were no graves in Egypt, hast thou taken us away to die in the wilderness? wherefore hast thou dealt thus with us, to carry us forth out of Egypt? (Exod. 14:8-11).

It's amazing how many of us will be happy with the devil's junk because we don't want to pursue something that represents a challenge to us. We'd rather be in neutral than to face a challenge. We're reluctant to move out in God and face the enemy. It's easier for us to stay in bondage than to fight our way free, and too often in spiritual matters we choose the devil's comforts over God's best.

THE LORD WILL FIGHT FOR YOU

Is not this the word that we did tell thee in Egypt, saying, Let us alone, that we may serve the Egyptians? [Here comes the voice of the past.] For it had been better for us to serve the Egyptians, than that we should die in the wilderness. And Moses said unto the people, Fear ye not, stand still, and see the salvation of the LORD, which he will shew to you today: for the Egyptians whom ye have seen today, ye shall see them again no more for ever. The LORD shall fight for you, and ye shall hold your peace (Exod. 14:12-14).

When Moses said, "Stand still, and see the salvation of the LORD," he believed what he was saying, but he did not know what was going to happen. He didn't realize all the implications of what he had said. It was an expression of real faith. But then Moses apparently

201

tried to back a bit out of the leadership position and power that God had given him. He prayed for God to do something about the situation, and God got upset with his continued wavering and said, ". . . Wherefore criest thou unto me? speak unto the children of Israel, that they go forward" (Exod. 14:15). In other words, "Moses, stop looking to me for solutions I've already put in your hands. Take your position and lead my people forward."

Moses probably wondered, "Forward where? Does He know what's ahead of us? The Red Sea!" But Moses' bad memory—and the desperate urgency of doing something "right now!"—had made him forget that the LORD had given him "the rod of God." So God reminded him:

> But lift thou up thy rod, and stretch out thine hand over the sea, and divide it: and the children of Israel shall go on dry ground through the midst of the sea. [In other words, "I'm not going to part the Red Sea— you part it. I've given you the power to do it."] And I, behold, I will harden the hearts of the Egyptians, and they shall follow them: [I will make them so mad they'll follow you right through the sea] and I will get me honour upon Pharaoh, and upon all his host, upon his chariots, and upon his horsemen. And the Egyptians shall know that I am the LORD, when I have gotten me honour upon Pharaoh, upon his chariots, and upon his horsemen (Exod. 14: 16-18).

Moses obeyed God and "Stretched out his hand over the sea; and the LORD caused the sea to go back by a strong east wind all that night, and made the sea dry land, and the waters were divided (Exod. 14:21).

What a miracle! The Lord caused the sea to go back. This miracle enabled the children of Israel to go across on dry ground. The Egyptians pursued them into the middle of the sea, the waters surged back and all the Egyptians drowned.

Moses' song of deliverance tells the story of God's power and glory in delivering His people from their enemies:

> And in the greatness of thine excellency thou hast overthrown them that rose up against thee: thou sentest forth thy wrath, which consumed them as stubble. And with the blast of thy nostrils the waters were gathered together, the floods stood upright as an heap, and the depths were congealed in the heart of the sea. The enemy said, I will pursue, I will overtake, I will divide the spoil; my lust shall be satisfied upon them; I will draw my sword, my hand shall destroy them. Thou didst blow with thy wind, the sea covered them: they sank as lead in the mighty waters. Who is like unto thee, O LORD, among the gods? who is like thee, glorious in holiness, fearful in praises, doing wonders? (Exod. 15:7-11).

Psalm 29 paints the picture of God's power even more vividly:

> Give unto the LORD, O ye mighty, give unto the LORD glory and strength. Give unto the LORD the glory due unto his name; worship the LORD in the beauty of holiness. *The voice of the LORD* is upon the waters: the God of glory thundereth: the LORD is upon many waters. *The voice of the LORD* is powerful; the voice of the LORD is full of majesty....

The LORD sitteth upon the flood; yea, the LORD sitteth King for ever. The LORD will give strength unto his people; the LORD will bless his people with peace (Ps. 29:1-4; 10-11, italics mine).

The power of the voice of the Lord (His breath, His Word, His Spirit) has no equal anywhere. Isaiah said that the enemy will come in like a flood, but the Spirit of the Lord shall raise up a standard against him. When the waters needed to be divided, Moses stretched forth the rod, and God spoke to the wind. The waters of the sea, seventy-five feet deep, congealed like jello. That's the power God sometimes puts in the hands of those He calls, and the power of His Word.

THE POWER OF OUR WORDS

Where did Elihu say the words of such power came from? There is a spirit in man. In effect, he said, "This spirit in man makes me full of words. The spirit in man gives me understanding. It makes unwise men wise. It even separates a supposedly wise man from the world. The world says that great men are wise, but great men are not always wise. I am full of matter by the Spirit of God. This spirit is bringing me such force that I have to let these words out."

Where is the Spirit of the Lord? He's in me. He's in you. The Spirit of the Lord is within us. How do I get the Spirit of the Lord within me to such an extent that His Word gets to my mouth? By studying the Word of God. When I build my house on this Rock, I am a wise man. I am practical.

The Rock is the Word of God. I put the Word in me, and the Word, by the Spirit in me, constrains me. That Word comes up into my mouth and I begin to speak it. My word will drive back the enemy. This is the standard that the Lord has raised against him.

The breath of Almighty God goes out against the devil. How? God can do it. It happened when He placed His Spirit within us. The anointing that abides in us (1 John 2:27) teaches us all things. We take the Word of the Lord; we put it in our mouth; we begin to speak the Word of the Lord—and the enemy is driven back. When I speak His Word, it is the same as if the Lord were speaking, if my life is in order before Him.

Therefore, be a wise person and build your house on the Rock.

The floods will come, the winds will blow, the rains will descend, but your house will not move.

16

God Is Good All the Time

There's a bumper sticker that says, "God Is Good All the Time." I really like its positive confession. No matter how tough the times may get, the tough people of God hold onto the truth that God is good.

Everything God does is based on His character. God is not trying to love—He *is* love. We are commanded to love, but God is love all the time. God's character is love. It is not difficult for Him to love us, even when we behave in ugly ways.

Most of us try to earn what God gives. That's why many of our fundamentalist roots, deeply planted in the soil of the churches we came out of, were erroneous and wrong. Very little was based on grace. Everything was based on works. Consequently, if you wore earrings, you weren't holy. I've never understood what earrings have to do with holiness. Our whole focus was on works, and on outward appearances rather than inner qualities.

In Romans 11, we read about the grafting of the Gentile branch of the Church into the vine. Paul is clearly identifying the fact that we, as Gentiles, were not originally chosen in God's plan. God grafted us in afterward because of His mercy, grace and love. This enabled Gentiles to be a part of the great family of God.

> For I speak to you Gentiles, inasmuch as I am the apostle of the Gentiles, I magnify mine office [In other words, he was happy to be in the office he had]: If by any means I may provoke to emulation [to copy] them which are my flesh [As I am a Jew, I wish these other Jews that are like me would copy what I am doing], and might save some of them. For if the casting away of them be the reconciling of the world [In other words, because God chose to bring in the Gentiles. By casting away we are talking about changing His direction from them, not casting them away forever, but for the time being], what shall the receiving of them be, but life from the dead? (Rom. 11:13-15).

In other words, these things will take place when they become a part of what God's plan is—to bring the Gentile branch or wing of believers in. The previous exclusivity enjoyed by the Jews is no longer the case under God's grace. God's plan of salvation, as it is revealed in the New Testament, is for all people who believe. This is the reason why I have a difficult time hearing someone say, "I'm a fulfilled Jew."

Becoming a child of God has nothing to do with your ethnic background. In Jesus Christ there is no color, no creed, no background. Everything in Jesus has to do with a new creation. I am a Christian. I am fulfilled in Jesus Christ. That is the whole plan of God for me and for the world.

208

BECAUSE OF FAITH

> And if some of the branches be broken off, and
> thou, being a wild olive tree, wert grafted in among
> them, and with them partakest of the root and fatness
> of the olive tree; boast not against the branches . . ."
> (Rom. 11:17-18).

In this passage, Paul is talking to the Gentiles. He is
telling them that the reason they are in the vine now is
because the natural branches were broken off (the natural
branches being the Jews), and the Gentiles were grafted
in. In effect, the great Apostle Paul is saying, "Don't
boast in yourself. You were not the original branches.
You were grafted in. You are a part of God's covenant
of grace."

> Boast not against the branches. But if thou boast,
> thou bearest not the root, but the root thee. Thou wilt
> say then, The branches were broken off, that I might
> be grafted in. Well; *because of unbelief they were
> broken off, and thou standest by faith.* Be not
> highminded, but fear . . . (Rom. 11:18-20, italics mine).

God did not just come along and say, "I don't want
those Jews to be a part of my olive tree anymore." It was
their decision to walk in unbelief that caused them to be
broken off. Here, we are certainly not talking about every
individual Jew. We are talking about a nation disobeying
God. He said they were broken off because of unbelief,
"But thou standest by faith."

"Be not highminded, but fear." Have awesome
respect, be filled with reverence for God. If the Jewish

nation was broken off because of unbelief, the only way the Gentiles will be able to stand is by faith. The possibility exists that you will be broken off, too, if you don't stand in faith, but get into unbelief as they did.

It amuses me to see people fighting against the faith message. Some people even say, "Well, the faith movement is dead." Faith isn't a movement—it's a life-style. A movement is something that happens for a while and then passes away. The Bible says, "But without faith it is impossible to please God" (Heb. 11:6). Your background has little to do with it. You could have been a member of any denomination—it doesn't matter. Faith brings us together.

This doesn't mean we're pushing faith. God is pushing faith. Without faith it is impossible to please Him

Paul said that the Gentiles stood because of their faith. When the Jews got into unbelief, they were cast off. He also told the Gentiles that they had better have reverence and not be high-minded, thinking that they were somebodies in themselves, because they were not.

"For if God spared not the natural branches, take heed lest he also spare not thee" (Rom. 11:21). In the same way that Israel, the nation God raised up, lost the privilege of covenant, so will we lose the privilege of covenant if we don't stand in faith.

> Behold therefore the goodness and severity of God: on them which fell, severity; but toward thee, goodness, if thou continue in his goodness: otherwise thou also shalt be cut off. And they also, if they abide not still in unbelief, shall be grafted in: for God is able to graft them in again (Rom. 11:22-23).

In effect, Paul is saying, "You need to understand the character of the God we are serving." God will allow what you allow. He will permit what you permit. The Apostle Paul said that they could still get in if they would stop abiding in unbelief. He also pointed out that God has two sides. He is good to them who stand in faith, but He can be severe to those who disregard Him.

The two main things that will stop you from experiencing the goodness of God are unbelief and ignorance. There shouldn't be an ignorant person in the Church of Jesus Christ because the Bible reveals the "whole counsel of God". For most of us, therefore, our problem isn't ignorance—it's unbelief.

The disciples faced several great challenges. Once, for example, a demon-possessed person was brought to them. He threw himself on the ground, foamed at the mouth, and gnashed with his teeth. They were trying to cast the devil out of him, but in frustration they said that they couldn't do it. They got Jesus alone and asked him, "Why could not we cast him out?" (Matt. 17:19).

Jesus told them, "Because of your unbelief."

A doctrine has been built on the fact that Jesus went on to say, "Howbeit this kind goeth not out but by prayer and fasting" (Matt. 17:21). The doctrine tells us that the only way you can get demon-possessed people free from demons is by fasting. That's not what the Scripture says. The Scripture says they could not cast the demon out because of unbelief. Jesus then went on to describe that this kind of problem has to be dealt with spiritually. The principle of growing strong in God is built on prayer and fasting.

"Behold, the goodness and the severity of God." The

goodness of God is for those who stand in faith. The severity of God is for those who don't care—they stand in unbelief and disregard God's Word.

What's a simple definition of faith? It's believing that something which you don't see, feel or understand in the natural really exists. Realize what faith is *not*. It is not sense knowledge. It's not cognitive understanding.

The goodness of God is reserved for those who stand in faith. God has everything we need, but until we begin, by faith, to reach out to Him, everything He has will stay where He is.

We sometimes hear expressions like the following: "If God is so good, how come Sister So-and-So is like she is?"

Sister So-and-So may love God; she may even have served God for years, but she doesn't know what her rights are. Her situation is like you having a rich uncle who died and left you a million dollars, but no one ever told you about it. You could have a million dollars in your name, but unless someone comes to your door, calls you on the phone or sends you a Federal Express message and lets you know, you could remain poor.

"The LORD is my shepherd; *I shall not want"* (Ps. 23:1, italics mine). This passage doesn't say anything about needs. The Bible is full of the doctrine that tell us that God wants to meet your wants as well as your needs. Faith people are often criticized as follows: "All you people think about is material needs and getting things from God." This is God's promise to us. He's our loving Father and He wants to bless us. He is good all the time.

The rest of Psalm 23 is so beautiful—it describes green pastures, still waters, the restoration of the soul, leading in the paths of righteousness, goodness and mercy and eternal life. It declares that even when I walk through the valley of the shadow of death, I will not fear evil. He will be and always is with me. His rod and staff will comfort me. He prepares a table before me in the presence of my enemy. This is prosperity. He anoints my head with oil. My cup runs over!

> Surely goodness and mercy shall follow me all the days of my life: and I will dwell in the house of the LORD for ever (Ps. 23:6).

God uses the word surely. It means positively, absolutely, beyond question, beyond a doubt. It is surely, not possibly. This is not possibility thinking, it's God's promise to us. Surely, without a doubt, goodness and mercy are ours.

We don't have to pursue goodness. We don't have to pursue mercy. We don't have to pursue the good things of God. They automatically follow us. We don't even have to confess these blessings every day. In fact, the more you know about the goodness of God, the less you have to confess it. My purpose in life is not to tap into His goodness, it is to tap into His righteousness. When I tap into His righteousness and holiness, His goodness follows me. IT FOLLOWS ME!

Wherever I go, I ought to be taking goodness with me. Two twins follow me wherever I go—their names are goodness and mercy. Everywhere I go, as a child of God, I take mercy and goodness with me. They are my constant companions. "Come on, Goodness and Mercy," I say, and they follow me ALL the days of my life.

The Bible says that I "will dwell in the house of the LORD for ever" Wherever I go, the presence of God is with me. The presence of God is with me, and it represents the character of God. The character of God is goodness.

I had one of the best fathers who ever lived. He's in heaven now. I could never conceive of my earthly father saying to me, "Son, I love you so much, I'm going to pray that God gives you a tumor."

"Son, I love you so much, I'm going outside to cut your brake linings. When you go a mile or two and then put your foot on the brake, you'll have a terrible accident. That's how much I love you. I want you to have an accident so you'll learn some important things."

That's how some people think about our heavenly Father. That's not the God described by the Psalmist: "Goodness and mercy shall follow me all the days of my life."

THE DOCTRINE OF NO WANT

The Psalmist knew God. To him, God was always good:

> I will bless the LORD at all times: his praise shall continually be in my mouth. My soul shall make her boast in the LORD: the humble shall hear thereof, and be glad. O magnify the LORD with me, and let us exalt his name together. I sought the LORD, and he heard me, and delivered me from all my fears. They looked unto him, and were lightened: and their faces were not ashamed. This poor man cried, and the LORD heard him, and saved him out of all his troubles (Ps. 34:1-6).

This poor man cried, and the Lord heard him and saved him out of all his troubles. I can hear David crying out to God from his heart:

> The angel of the LORD encampeth round about them that fear him, and delivereth them. O taste and see that the LORD is good: blessed is the man that trusteth in him. O fear the LORD, ye his saints: for there is no want to them that fear him (Ps. 34:7-9).

This says no want—it doesn't say even talk about need. This is stated clearly. We could even call this the *Doctrine of No Want.* It is clearly signified in many Scriptures: Ps. 23:1, Ps. 84:11, Ps. 91:1-12, Ps. 103:3, Matt. 21:22, Mark 9:23, and Mark 11:22-24. These are just a few of the many passages that teach that God's people—the people of faith—will not want.

The Bible says that every word must be established out of the mouth of two or three witnesses. Nine of these scriptural words are cited above. There are actually twenty-five passage that teach the *Doctrine of No Want.* The Scriptures do not say "no need," because the Bible says our heavenly Father knows what you have need of.

You need to memorize Matthew 6 so that it will get so deeply imbedded in your thinking that you will never have to pray again for clothes, for a place to live or for food. Some of you are wasting your time confessing about clothes, food and a house. Don't do that. The Bible says that your heavenly Father knows what you have need of. Those things are needs. Need is a house. Need is food. Need is clothing. Want, on the other hand, is a good house. Want is a good car. Want is good food.

I can almost hear someone beginning to accuse:

"You people are so materialistically minded!" No. We are God-covenant-minded.

> The young lions do lack, and suffer hunger: but they that seek the LORD shall not want any good thing (Ps. 34:10).

The young lion is always on the prowl. He's aggressive. He threateningly growls and he's ferocious. He doesn't have a full understanding of how to get his food. In fact, the young male lion never hunts. It's the female that does the hunting. She makes a little growl—all the young lions come. Then old papa comes along.

The young lions suffer hunger. They have to be taught how to get their own food. In other words, it doesn't make a difference how smart you look, how tough you seem, how loud you growl, how aggressive you appear to be, the principle is that you have to seek the Lord. When you seek the Lord, good things come to you. When you seek the Lord, you don't lack any good thing.

The first year of our marriage, my wife and I had to pay a lot of taxes. I was angry about it. My wife Diane turned to me and said, "If you don't like paying such high taxes, then you shouldn't be making this much money."

I said, "You know what? Paying these taxes is a good thing."

I had been complaining, and Diane reminded me, "You're missing it. Paying more taxes means you're receiving more blessings."

Paying taxes, therefore, is a blessing even though I don't like the way they use my tax dollars. That's not my responsibility, however. My responsibility is to render unto Caesar the things that are his, and unto God the things that are His. We seek God, not the blessings, and the blessings follow.

People have asked me, "Did you confess your way into what you have?"

This answer is no, not really. Goodness and mercy simply follow me everywhere I go. Recently, for example, I went up to a counter in a department store with a shirt I liked, and the saleslady said, "This one is twenty-five percent off the lowest ticketed price." That's goodness and mercy following me. When I seek the Lord, I don't want for any good thing.

> Come, ye children, hearken unto me: I will teach you the fear of the LORD. What man is he that desireth life, and loveth many days, that he may see good? (Ps. 34:11-12).

The desires (wants) that the Psalmist refers to are common aspirations of mankind. They are God's desires for us as well.

> Keep thy tongue from evil, and thy lips from speaking guile. Depart from evil, and do good; seek peace, and pursue it. The eyes of the LORD are upon the righteous, and his ears are open unto their cry (Ps. 34:13-15).

God, in effect, is saying, "Yes, I see it. Angels—go right there. There's that believing guy. There's that righteous guy. Go bless him. Go bless him. Put my blessings on him."

God is looking—His ears are open unto their cry.
God sees us.
He loves us.
He hears us.
He blesses us.

17

God Blesses All the Time

> The face of the LORD is against them that do evil, to cut off the remembrance of them from the earth. The righteous cry, and the LORD heareth, and delivereth them out of all their troubles. The LORD is nigh unto them that are of a broken heart; and saveth such as be of a contrite spirit. Many are the afflictions of the righteous: but *the LORD delivereth him out of them all* (Ps. 34:16-19, italics mine).

DELIVERETH OUT OF THEM ALL!

I get letters from people that say, "Ever since I started serving the Lord, ever since I started to tithe, it seems like all hell broke loose against my finances. Can you tell me, Pastor, why is this happening?"

I answer them along the following lines: Do you think the devil is going to get off your back because you made a decision to serve God? The fact that you made a decision to serve God put you in a position as open

219

prey for him. He wants you to be discouraged. He wants you to doubt, and he wants you to talk negative to everyone you meet. "I went to that church over there, and all they ever talk about is blessings and covenant, blessings and covenant. I've been there six months and nothing good has ever happened to me."

With that attitude, I wouldn't bless you if I were God, either. We want to use "spiritual situational ethics." We say, "I've been trusting God and confessing the Word but nothing has happened to me. What do you think the answer is, Pastor?"

Are we obeying the Word? "Having done all, STAND!" Some of us have been on the brink of a miracle and we gave up just before it was ready to explode on our behalf.

"Well, I've been trusting the Lord for this thing to happen for five years." You haven't been trusting Him for five years. You can tell that to me, but let me see you tell that to God with a straight face.

People tell me, "But, I've been standing on the Word of God." You haven't been standing on the Word of God if you're discouraged. When you're standing on the Word of God, you don't get discouraged. You get encouraged.

"I've been trusting God." When you trust God, you get stronger.

"Bless God, I'm standing on the Word of God, Pastor, but nothing is happening." When you're standing on the Word of God, something is happening. When you're standing on your emotions, however, that's an entirely different story.

We say, "I thank you, Father God, in the name of

Jesus, that I'm the healed of God. I thank you that I walk in divine prosperity," but we don't even know what we're saying.

> How amiable are thy tabernacles, O LORD of hosts! My soul longeth, yea, even fainteth for the courts of the LORD [I wonder how many of us really love God that much]: my heart and my flesh crieth out for the living God. Yea, the sparrow hath found an house, and the swallow a nest for herself, where she may lay her young, even thine altars, O LORD of hosts, my King, and my God. Blessed are they that dwell in thy house: they will be still praising thee. Selah [Pause and think]. Blessed is the man whose strength is in thee; in whose heart are the ways of them (Ps. 84:1-5).

The blessings of God come to those who live in His presence, to those who find their strength in Him:

"Who passing through the valley of Baca make it a well; the rain also filleth the pools" (Ps. 84:6) This is referring to the valley of sorrow and weeping. The word "well" means springs. The people who serve God can make a spring in the desert.

"They go from strength to strength, every one of them in Zion appeareth before God" (Ps. 84:7). God says, "I'm going to take you from strength to strength." In other words, you're not as strong as God wants you to be yet.

> O LORD God of hosts, hear my prayer: give ear, O God of Jacob. Selah. Behold, O God our shield, and look upon the face of thine anointed. For a day in thy

courts is better than a thousand. I had rather be a doorkeeper in the house of my God, than to dwell in the tents of wickedness (Ps. 84:8-10).

God is our shield. In His presence there is fullness of joy "For the LORD God is a sun and shield: the LORD will give grace and glory: *no good thing will he withhold from them that walk uprightly*" (Ps. 84:11, italics mine).

Are you are starting to get the picture that God is saying, "I want to bless you. I want to bless you, my son and my daughter." He will give grace and glory. In fact, He will not withhold any good thing from you.

> Bless the LORD, O my soul: and all that is within me, bless his holy name. Bless the LORD, O my soul, and forget not all his benefits (Ps. 103:1-2).

When an insurance salesman tries to sell insurance, he doesn't tell his prospective customer all the bad things about the insurance. He emphasizes the good things. He would never say, "Let me tell you why you should buy this insurance. You should buy this insurance because it never really pays at the end. In fact, you lose money during the whole term of the insurance. In fact, it's a real risk."

You would never try to sell something in that way. It would be like a vacuum cleaner salesperson knocking at your door and saying, "See this vacuum cleaner? You need to buy this. It's not a very good machine, it doesn't even pick up lint. The bags only last two hours. It also breaks down a lot, but I think you ought to buy it."

A salesperson always stresses the benefits of the product or service. They say, "This is the reason you ought to buy this. Look at the benefits."

All too often, with children, we take the negative approach. We may warn them, "Be careful when you cross the road. That car will kill you if you don't watch out." Instead, we should say, "That's a red light. That's a green light. When it's green, it's your turn to go across." This is teaching—it requires patience and thoroughness.

It's ineffective to say, "Put that jacket on. You'll catch your death of cold." This programs the wrong message into their minds. Too many people see God as a negative, critical parent. The world thinks God always has a negative attitude and is usually angry as well. Why? Because the Church has presented Him that way.

Some television preachers reinforce this negative view of God. A man stands there and preaches, "If you don't accept Jesus, you're going to burn in hell!" We have become so hell-conscious that the world only knows the Christian Church as a place where hellfire and brimstone are emphasized. God is good all the time, God blesses all the time.

> Bless the LORD, O my soul: and all that is within me, bless his holy name. Bless the LORD, O my soul, and forget not all his benefits: Who forgiveth all thine iniquities; who healeth all thy diseases; who redeemeth thy life from destruction; who crowneth thee with lovingkindness and tender mercies; who satisfieth thy mouth with good things; so that thy youth is renewed like the eagle's. The LORD executeth righteousness and judgment for all that are oppressed (Ps. 103:1-6).

In other words, God is saying, "I know when you're in deep trouble. I'll take care of you. Don't try to fight your own way out." This is so contrary to the way most of us were taught as children. We were taught that we had to fight our own battles. God says, "Stop fighting your own battles. Now that you serve me, I'll fight them for you."

> He made known his ways unto Moses, his acts
> unto the children of Israel (Ps. 103:7).

We, as God's children, should not have to hinge our faith on His acts. When you know His ways, you leave His acts up to Him. "His ways" means His character. His acts are the little fringe benefits. I don't want the fringe benefits. I want the Benefactor.

Moses knew His ways, but the children of Israel knew Him only by His acts. Moses knew God. He knew how God would react in every circumstance. Some of us have relegated our relationship with God to things. Our relationship with God is based on His acts.

We cry, "O, God, I need help. I'm in deep trouble." Then God helps us and we say, "Thanks, God. See you next year." If this is your approach, next year the Bible might turn back at you. The face of the Lord is against the unrighteous.

We wonder why we don't see the goodness of God. It's because a lot of us have a religion based on acts. We don't really know God. That's why some people are critical of faith people. A lot of faith people have a religion of the mouth. Such "faith people" have made themselves open game to the attacks of others.

Faith is not works. It's not based on our works or on God's works. Faith is based on trust. It's trust in God's grace. Faith works, but works are not faith.

The Bible says do not forget ALL of His benefits. God wants to bless me, but He wants to bless me on the basis of a relationship that is right.

> If ye be willing and obedient, ye shall eat the good of the land: but if ye refuse and rebel, ye shall be devoured with the sword: for the mouth of the LORD hath spoken it (Isa. 1:19-20).

If you're willing and obedient, you'll eat the good of the land. There must be some bad in the land along with the good. Most of us have experienced enough tough times in our lifetimes that we are tired of them and from now on we want to experience good things.

> And we know [We are not thinking about it, trying to figure it out.] that all things work together for good to them that love God, to them who are the called according to his purpose (Rom. 8:28).

The Phillips translation says that all things fit into a pattern for good.

The problem with many of us relates to the fast-paced society in which we live. If things have not gone well for us this week, and we're a little discouraged or depressed, we say, "I thought God was good." We live in a space-time age. Everything is related to what we're feeling NOW. We don't seem to grab hold of the fact that what I'm experiencing now in the present has nothing to do with the eternal purpose of God in my life and the destiny that God has for me. We have a problem with seeing the total picture.

We may say, "Oh, I thought that God healed," when an expected healing does not occur. That's not the appropriate response. We should say, "Devil you're a liar! I am NOT destined to be crippled for the rest of my life."

"All things work together for good to them that love God . . ." (Rom. 8:28). They really do. All things, not just some. Moses knew God's ways. Any person who knows God's ways will say, "It doesn't make any difference that I have to be out here forty years. Lord, you told me I was the deliverer of Israel. It doesn't make a difference that my beard is getting gray and my back is hurting me. It doesn't matter that things are looking so bad. I know that one of these days, you'll summon me. When you do, Lord, I'll be ready."

Finally, at the age of eighty, Moses became the deliverer of Israel. He wasn't worried about his age. He wasn't even worried about his reputation. He was a murderer—the Church probably would have excommunicated him.

At eighty years of age, Moses was tending sheep. God so much as told him, "Your time is up, son." Moses knew His ways: he knew that his heavenly Father would never leave him or forsake him. Like Moses, let your heart remain fixed.

All things work together for good. I want you to get hold of the word GOOD. God is good all the time—and God blesses us all the time.

Ask, and it shall be given you; seek, and ye shall find; knock, and it shall be opened unto you: For every

one that asketh receiveth; and he that seeketh findeth;
and to him that knocketh it shall be opened (Matt. 7:7-8).

This doesn't sound like the God who used to be taught to me. I used to think that you had to beg God for blessings: "Oh, Lord, I'm your humble servant. I'm over here just crying out to you."

Jesus tells us to, "Relax, just ask and you shall receive. Seek and you shall find. Knock and it shall be opened unto you. Everyone that asks receives; and to everyone that knocks, it shall be opened."

"Or what man is there of you, whom if his son ask bread, will he give him a stone?" (Matt. 7:9).

"Mommy, I'm hungry!"

"Here! Have these fresh-baked rocks."

"Daddy, I love you."

"Come over here," the father says as he whacks the kid on the back of the head. "Don't say that to me anymore!"

As ridiculous as it seems, that's the way we think about God. We see God standing there and saying, "I can't wait to punish you. I can't wait to get my hands on you. I'm going to squeeze you. I want your arm hanging off in a wreck. I want you bloody." That's not the good God we serve.

"Or if he ask a fish, will he give him a serpent? If ye then, being evil, know how to give good gifts unto your children, *how much more shall your Father which is in heaven give good things to them that ask him?"* (Matt. 7:10-11, italics mine). All we have to do is ask in faith, nothing wavering.

"If ye abide in me, and my words abide in you, ye

shall ask what ye will, and it shall be done unto you" (John 15:7). That simple statement blows away the whole theory of begging God as follows, "Lord, if it be thy will . . . ." Such a prayer is actually a prayer of unbelief, especially if we are praying something to God that already is His will.

It sounds good, religious and pious, but it's junk. God said, "I am the Lord that healeth thee" (Exod. 15:26). He did not say "sometimes." It was the church that taught us that He heals sometimes. God has been trying to tell us, "I'm the Lord that heals you. My name is I AM, not I WAS."

God said, "Bring ye all the tithes into the storehouse . . . and prove me . . . if I will not open you the windows of heaven, and pour you out a blessing that there shall not be room enough to receive it" (Mal. 3:10). That's what God said. He said it's yours. All you have to do is trust and obey His Word by being willing and obedient. Your part is willingness and obedience—He'll do the rest.

Jesus said, "If you abide in Me, and My words abide in you, you ask what you will, and it shall be done unto you." He wants His words to take up residence within our hearts.

> Do not err, my beloved brethren. Every good gift and every perfect gift is from above, and cometh down from the Father of lights, with whom is no variableness, neither shadow of turning" (James 1:16-17).

If every good gift and every perfect gift comes from above, where do the tough times and the challenges come from? From below. Bad things come from below. And all along, we've been blaming God above for the bad things. He's our heavenly Father, the Giver of every good and perfect gift. Every perfect gift is from above.

Some lingering doubts and religious ideas remain embedded in people's minds. Even though they'd never believe that God is evil, they can't accept the fact that He's really good. They are suspect. You can't have any doubt about God and expect Him to bless you. You can't waver. As James points out: "A double minded man is unstable in all his ways" (James 1:8).

The Bible says that Israel was cut off because of their unbelief. The branch was cut off. Through the Apostle Paul, God said that He was going to graft in a Gentile branch that is going to believe me." Realizing this, Paul told us not to get high-minded, because if we don't stand in faith, we're going to be cut off too.

The reason why some people today are staying in tough times is because they don't truly believe the Word of God.

Are you ready to believe a good God who always wants to bless His people?

Tough times demand tough people who rise up in faith to fully know that their God is good all the time.

He never changes.

He will lead you through the flood, the storm, the fire, the earthquake.

He's a good God who wants to bless you all the time.

"O taste and see that the Lord is good . . ." (Ps. 34:8).